To those who agree that

THE PROPER STUDY OF

MANKIND IS FOOD

this book is dedicated

The Act of Eating, which hath by several wise Men been considered as extremely mean and derogatory, . . . must be in some Measure performed by the greatest Prince, Heroe, or Philosopher upon Earth.

Henry Fielding, *Tom Jones*

Dinner with Tom Jones

Eighteenth-century cookery adapted for the modern kitchen by

LORNA J. SASS

The Metropolitan Museum of Art

Other titles by Lorna J. Sass in The Metropolitan Museum of Art historical cookery series:

To the King's Taste: Richard II's book of feasts and recipes adapted for modern cooking

To the Queen's Taste: Elizabethan feasts and recipes adapted for modern cooking

LIBRARY OF CONGRESS CATALOGING IN PUBLICATION DATA
Sass, Lorna J
  Dinner with Tom Jones.

  Bibliography: p.
  Includes index.
  1. Cookery, English. I. Title

TX717.S318   641.5'942   77-24494
ISBN 0-87099-167-1

Designed by Peter Oldenburg
Composition by Custom Composition Co.
Printed by Eastern Press
Bound by A. Horowitz & Son

Table of Contents

WHO CAN HEAR the name Tom Jones without smiling and calling to mind that unforgettable scene in the film version of the novel: Tom and Mrs. Waters sitting at the "Table of Love," sloshing oysters down their gullets, gnawing roasted meat from colossal bones, and all the time devouring each other with their eyes. Indeed, the action of *Tom Jones* is punctuated by meals, and many a shoulder of mutton and tankard of ale are consumed by the time we reach the final course of Fielding's prose banquet.

In the novel, Fielding describes people eating simple fare; and foreign travelers visiting Georgian England report that "two dishes are their Dinners; a Pudding for instance, and a Piece of roast Beef." Since the "roast beef of old England" is by now a culinary cliché, this description comes as no surprise to us.

What may surprise, though, is the fact that roasts and puddings constituted only part of the gastronomic picture. Examining English cookbooks published between 1700 and 1760 (roughly the span of Henry Fielding's lifetime), I was intrigued to discover that recipes for French *ragoo* and *friggassee* were offered side by side with instructions for making such traditional English dishes as *collar'd mutton* and Yorkshire pudding. Furthermore, many cookbooks contained elaborate diagrams depicting elegant menus and fashionable ways to present the various courses of the meal. Assured that some of my ancestors did, in fact, manage to escape their reputed culinary monotony, I found myself visualizing Tom Jones, that Epicurean *par excellence,* savoring the bounty of those sophisticated meals.

Hence, the evolution of this cookbook—a celebration of the hearty English and delicate French dishes that often stood side by side on the Georgian table. Won't you join me for *Dinner with Tom Jones?*

LORNA J. SASS

Acknowledgments

GENEROUS FRIENDS and colleagues, cooks and scholars have contributed to the making of *Dinner with Tom Jones.* My thanks to:

Robie Rogge, of the Metropolitan Museum, for her king-size enthusiasm and her queenly quest for perfection . . . Peter Oldenburg, designer, for a vision that enhances my own . . . Shari Lewis, for her sensitive and patient editing of the text . . .

10

Osa Brown, for the equanimity and efficiency with which she took this book through production . . . Clare LeCorbeiller, for showing me the Museum's fascinating collection of eighteenth-century porcelain . . . W. S. Lewis, for sharing with me his magnificent collection of period prints . . . James Trager, for permission to quote from *The Food Book* in my dedication . . . Professors James Clifford, John Middendorf, and Howard Schless, of Columbia University, for their valuable comments on the Introduction . . . Lon Rosenfield, for sharing with me his ideas about the novel . . . Professor Frank Melton, for suggesting worthwhile bibliography on eighteenth-century social history . . . Louis Szathmary, for inviting me to work in his archives . . . Columbia Professor Robert Hanning, for offering unwavering support and encouragement to this medievalist errant . . . The Flour Advisory Board in London, for advice during the "seed-cake crisis," and especially Audrey Ellison, for help and favors too numerous to mention . . . Elizabeth David, for providing detailed information on the penny-loaf and early trifle . . . Marian Bush, Joyce Curwin, Carol Flechner, Aileen Hall, Jean Mandelbaum, Deborah Signer, Maida Silverman, and Michelle Urvater, for reading the text and trying many of the recipes . . . Edith Sailon and Eleanor Sass, for being adventurous cooks . . . My friends, for being critical tasters at Sunday-night dinners.

. . . We think it not Disparagement to our Heroe to mention the immoderate Ardour with which he laid about him at this Season. Indeed it may be doubted, whether Ulysses, . . . in that eating Poem of the Odyssey, ever made a better Meal. Three Pounds at least of that Flesh which formerly had contributed to the Composition of an Ox, was now honoured with becoming Part of the individual Mr. Jones.

Henry Fielding, *Tom Jones*

H. Fielding

Introduction

Tom Jones was born in the Pudding Age, when the expression "to come in pudding-time" meant to arrive at the luckiest moment in the world. And so he did.

During the first half of the eighteenth century, England was the granary of Europe. Food production exceeded need; even the peasantry had access to quality meat and fine wheat bread.[1] Daniel Defoe, one of the keenest observers of the time, reports in his *Review of the State of the British Nation* (1709):

> Every single Person living at the common Rate of Plenty in England . . .
> consumes in Food two Quarters of Wheat, four Quarters of Barley, five Quarters
> of Peas or Beans Green, a Bullock, six Sheep, two Calves, and an Hog, and a
> hundred Pound of Butter, or Cheese, or Milk, in a Year; besides Fowls, Fish,
> Fruit, and Garden-Stuff.

Meat and produce were of superior quality, and it is therefore easy to accept travelers' claims that most Englishmen enjoyed simple fare. But among the urban gentry and an upward-reaching middle class, it became fashionable to reject native country cooking in favor of French and other exotic preparations.

> I hate everything that Old England brings forth, except it be the temper of an
> English Husband, and the liberty of an English wife; I love the French Bread,
> French Wines, French Sauces, and a French Cook; in short, I have all about me
> French or Foreign, from my Waiting Woman to my Parrot.
>
> *The English Lady's Catechism* (1703)

13

So prevalent were the lapses in gastronomic patriotism on certain English tables, that one gentleman feared resultant doom on the battlefield.

> It is not without the greatest Indignation that I see the surprising Regard which is paid to French Cookery at Present, that at the Tables of some of our oldest English Nobility, an English Dish can scarce find Admittance, and is look'd on only with Contempt. Cou'd the past Ages . . . bear to see a Sir Loin give Place to a Ragoute and a Leg of Mutton yield to a Soup Meagre? . . . I may safely venture to affirm that it is the Nature of the Inhabitants of this Isle to fight as they eat; and that it was from English Food that the Battles of Agincourt, Poitiers, Blenheim, and Ramilles, were got by the Valour of Englishmen.
>
> "Remember my English Lads," said the Colonel of the Grenadiers, "your Beef and your Pudding; march up and singe the Beards off them."

> Will Lovemeal, "Essay on Eating"
> *The Gentleman's Magazine* (August, 1736)

Georgian Fare

MEAT. "The Englishman is entirely carnivorous," claims the French traveler Zetzner. "He eats very little bread and calls himself very economical because he spares himself of soup and dessert, which circumstance made me remark that an English dinner is like eternity, it has no beginning and no end."[2]

Gallic sarcasm notwithstanding, meat certainly held a position of prominence on the Georgian table. A more objective traveler, Peter Kalm of Sweden, reports that "the

Englishmen understand almost better than any other people the art of properly roasting a joint. . . . Whether it is of Ox, Calf, Sheep, or Swine, [it] has a fatness and a delicious taste, either because of the excellent pasture . . . or some way of fattening the cattle known to the butchers alone."[3]

Fielding bears witness to his countrymen's reverence for the well-prepared roast:

> At [Curate Supple's] first Arrival, which was immediately before the Entrance of the Roast-beef, he had given an Intimation that he had brought some News with him, and was beginning to tell, that he came that Moment from Mr. Allworthy's, when the Sight of the Roast-beef struck him dumb, permitting him only to say Grace, and to declare, He must pay his Respect to the Baronet: For so he called the Sirloin. (141)[4]

Meat that wasn't roasted was most commonly boiled, and the traditional English methods of collaring (recipe, p. 80) and jugging still survived as part of *The Whole Duty of a Woman:*

> TO COLLAR A CALF'S HEAD
> Take it in the Skin, scald it, and cleave it down, and boil it 'tell the Bones will come easily away; pour over it some Vinegar, and season it with Mace, Pepper, & Salt, Sweet Herbs, Sage, and Lemon Pepper; strew all over the Inside of your Collar, and collar it as you do Brawn; boil it in Vinegar, Salt, Water, and Spice, and keep it in the same.

> HARES JUGGED
> Cut it into Pieces, half lard them, and season them; then have a Jug of Earth

15

with a large Mouth, put in your Hare with a Faggot of Herbs, and two Onions stuck with Cloves, cover it down close, that nothing gets in, and boil it in Water three Hours, then turn it out and serve away.

Noblemen who had French or foreign cooks, and those hosts who wished to entertain in the fashionably exotic manner, served such foods as *Kibbob of Lamb* and *Currey the Indian Way*. They frequently sampled Spanish *olios* and French *friggassees* (recipe, p. 86), *harricos* (recipe, p. 78), and *ragoos* (recipe, p. 134). Foreign recipes were often rather fussy to prepare, and called for such "heterogeneous mixtures" that the down-to-earth author of *The Good Housewife* was convinced they were injurious to the health. Here is the type of recipe that proved worrisome:

RAGOO FOR DUCK À LA BRAISE

It is made either with Veal or Lambs Sweetbread, . . . Cocks Combs, Mushrooms, Truffles, Asparagus Tops, and Artichoke Bottoms: Toss up all this in melted Bacon, moisten it with good Gravy, bind it with a Cullis of Veal and Ham, and when you have dished up your Duck, pour the Ragoo upon it.

The Whole Duty of a Woman

PUDDINGS. *"Blessed be He that Invented Pudding,* for it is a Manna that hits the Palates of all Sorts of People; a Manna, better than that of the Wilderness, because the People are never weary of it. Ah, what an excellent Thing is an English Pudding."[5]

Thus proclaims the French visitor Misson, continuing on a more sober note: "The Pudding is a Dish very difficult to be describ'd because of the several Sorts there are of it; . . . They bake them in an Oven, they boil them with Meat, they make them fifty several Ways." Judging by the recipes, puddings were prepared according to four main methods: boiling in a pudding cloth, cooking in a pot, baking in the oven, and frying in a dripping pan.

George I, the "Pudding King" (1714–1727), was served *plumb-pudding* (recipe, p. 108) at his first Christmas dinner in England. The main ingredients, currants and raisins, were bound together with a cake-like combination of bread crumbs, flour, milk, eggs, and suet. The mixture was highly spiced with ginger and nutmeg, then boiled in a floured pudding cloth for six to eight hours and served with a sauce of sack, sugar, and butter. Similar was *frute pudin*[g] (recipe, p. 114), except that in this dish the fruits were held together by a custard of sherry and eggs.

Some puddings were like the grain-thickened pottages of former times; one such was the "pudding in haste," or hasty pudding, of southern and midland England. It was prepared by boiling milk or cream in a large pot, then adding bread crumbs, flour, butter, eggs, dried fruits, spices, and sugar. The mixture was returned to the boil and stirred constantly until done. In this way a hasty pudding could be cooked in only thirty minutes, but the cook had to attend her pot very carefully if she did not want the pudding to scorch.

Puréed fruit puddings were often baked in puff-pastry crusts (recipe, p. 112), while more fanciful cooks recommended stuffing potato-sweetmeat pudding into bowls made of candied orange peel (recipe, p. 103). Artichoke and cauliflower puddings (recipes, pp. 104, 110) were baked with cream and spices in earthenware dishes, and sometimes served with wine-and-butter sauce.

Fried under the spit in the drippings that fell from roasting joints were the popular batter puddings made of milk, eggs, and flour. Of this type, Yorkshire pudding (recipes, p. 98) is probably the most familiar.

"Give an English Man a Pudding and he shall think it a noble Treat in any Part of the World," concludes Misson. What about the rest of us? You don't have to be English to love puddings.

FISH.   "Fish is dearer than any other Belly-timber at London," declares Misson, which is somewhat surprising, for the Thames was reputed to be overflowing with fish of all kinds. In fact, *The English Post* of June 5, 1702 reported that "a Sturgeon was taken the last Week in the River near Stepney, which the Lord Mayor sent as a Present to Her Majesty." Sturgeon, of course, was highly favored; its roe was pickled and the caviar served on toasted bread.

London's largest fish market was at Billingsgate, close to the river and its wharves; the stalls were open six days a week, except when the popular but exceptionally perishable mackerel was in season. (Mackerel was the only fish that could be sold legally on Sundays, before and after divine services.)

From London's markets fish was transported to the countryside, but ordering fish from afar was a risky business, as the following letters from Mr. Purefoy of Buckinghamshire to his fishmonger reveal:

> May 29, 1737: I was in hopes by this Time Mr. Ffisher would have sent some mackerell according to my order, but since none are come the weather is now so exceeding hot that what ffish you sent last week stank & could not be eat, so I desire you would not send any more fish till further orders. . . .
>
> March ye 12th, 1739: . . . Wee also rece[ive]d your kind present of a codling & oysters; the codling was very good, but the Oysters, half of them were as black as Ink & the other half was poisoned with the stench.[6]

Oysters, plentiful and exceedingly cheap, were sold from wheelbarrows along the streets for "Twelve Pence a Peck." The choicest were from Colchester and sold for three shillings a barrel. Large oysters were pickled, made into a *ragoo,* or used in stuffing (recipe, p. 88). The littlest ones were eaten raw, as the poet and playwright John Gay affectionately describes in *Trivia* (1716):

> If where Fleet Ditch with muddy Current flows,
> You chance to roam; Oyster Tubs in Rows
> Are rang'd beside the Posts; there stay thy Haste,
> And with the sav'ry Fish indulge thy Taste:
> The Damsel's Knife the gaping Shell commands,
> While the salt Liquor streams between her Hands.

Pickled and salted herring were much in demand. Defoe observes that in Norfolk alone, fifty thousand barrels of this cured fish were exported annually, "besides which, great

Quantities are brought in for the Consumption of the adjacent Country Towns."[7]

The well-stocked eighteenth-century kitchen had a good supply of anchovies, used extensively in cooking to impart flavor and to replace salt, which could be costly during this period. The solubility of anchovies made them convenient in sauce-making, and one thrifty cookbook writer even recommends frying anchovy bones in batter for a garnish.

FLORENTINES, PIES, AND TARTS.   Most cookery books give at least five or six recipes for making pie crusts. These *pastes,* as they were called, were often enriched with ground nuts (recipe, p. 166) or eggs (recipe, p. 162). According to Bradley, though, using eggs is "old fashion." In *The Country Housewife and Lady's Director,* he claims that "these are always hard, when they are baked, though they will fly and crackle in the Mouth, but they taste like Stickes." He recommends, instead, a sweet pastry of butter, flour, sugar, and sack or brandy (recipe, p. 164), concluding that "this is a very good one."

Puff pastry was much in vogue among those who affected French airs, but since butter was plentiful and thoroughly enjoyed, most English housewives probably knew how to make it. Here is Bradley's recipe. (It is virtually the same as Gervase Markham's recipe in *The English Hous-wife* [1615], and closely resembles our method of preparation today.)

> Rub in some Butter into your Flour, and make it into a Paste with Water, and when it is moulded, roll it out till it is about half an Inch thick; then put bits of Butter upon it, about a half an inch asunder, and fold your Paste together, and then fold it again: then roll it again till it becomes of the thickness it was before; and then lay bits of Butter on it, as before directed, and fold it as mentioned

above, and roll it again to the thickness of half an inch; then put on the rest of your Butter, and fold it up, and roll it for the last time, double it, and roll it twice before you use it.

Puff pastry was especially recommended for use as garniture. It was "cut in sprigs," baked in a gentle oven, and then glazed with egg whites. "So place and garnish your Dishes with it," directs one writer.

Except for the large freestanding "coffins" made of hot-water pastry (recipe, p. 160), pies were generally baked in decorative raised molds. The bottoms of these molds were elegantly carved so that when the pie or *florentine* (as it was also called) was turned out upside-down, the top crust would be sculpted. Cookbooks of the period are filled with plates showing suggested shapes for these raised pies: hearts, diamonds, trefoils, crosses.

Pies were filled with a wide assortment of ingredients, both sweet and savory: lamb, pigeon, duck, eggs and bacon, pork and apples (recipe, p. 76), mussels, flounder (recipe, p. 92), artichokes, and turtle. Mincemeat pie (recipe, p. 94) existed in many versions but almost always contained a mixture of minced meat, suet, and citrus peel. Christmas *mince pye* made a strong impression on Misson, who reports, "It is a great Nostrum of Composition . . . it is a most learned Mixture of Neats-tongues, Chicken, Eggs, Sugar, Raisins, Lemon and Orange Peel, various Kinds of Spicery, etc."

The distinction in terms is somewhat hazy, but pies were generally deep and covered, containing meat or fish, while tarts were shallow, open, and filled with sweet ingredients such as fruit (recipes, pp. 148, 152) or chocolate (recipe, p. 150). Pies were usually main dishes, while tarts were often served for "desart."

KITCHEN-GARDEN STUFF. For savory dishes, a wide variety of herbs was used. "You should always have them dry by you, kept in Paper Bags from the Dust," says Sarah Harrison in *The House-keeper's Pocket-Book,* "such as Red Sage, Thyme, Sweet-Marjoram, Mint, Pennyroyal, and all such other as you may want to season any Dish you are about to prepare."

Market gardens surrounded London, and, according to Kalm, "the vegetables which were most numerous . . . were beans, peas, cabbages of different sorts, leeks, chives, radishes, lettuce, asparagus [and] spinach." Vegetables were grown all year round, for in the winter these gardens were "covered over with glass frames . . . afterwards Russian matting over these, and straw over that four inches thick. . . . The Asparagus under them was one inch high, and considerably thick."

The largest market for fruits and vegetables was Covent Garden*, but peddlers sold slightly inferior produce throughout London, creating a cacophony of street cries which inspired Addison to suggest:

> I think it would be very proper that some Man of good Sense and sound Judgment should preside over these Publick Cries, who should permit none to lift up their Voices in our Streets, that have not tuneable Throats, and are not only able to overcome the Noise of the Crowd, and the rattling of Coaches, but also to vend their respective Merchandizes in apt Phrases, and in the most distinct and agreeable Sounds.

> *The Spectator*
> December 18, 1711

Mature root vegetables were stored for use in wheat straw. "The Skirret, thou' it is none of the largest Roots, yet is certainly one of the best Products of the Garden," claims the author of *The Whole Duty of a Woman,* who suggests that it be boiled and served with a sauce of butter, sack, and orange juice. The same preparation is recommended for the root vegetables salsify and scorzonera. Batty Langley, in *New Principles of Gardening* (1728), describes scorzonera as a "root almost like a Carrot [but] black without and white within,

* illustrated on the front endpapers

yielding a milky Juice." Roots grew to be extremely large: "I have had some Carrots," says Langley, ". . . that have been twenty-two inches in Length, and of twelve inches and a half Circumference at the greatest End." Root vegetables were often stewed in butter and cream (recipe, p. 106), or boiled and puréed for *soops* (recipe, p. 60) or *cullises* (recipe, p. 136).

For England, a relatively new and popular vegetable was celery. Langley claims, "There is no Herb adds so rich a Flavour to our Spring Sallets, as blanch'd Sellery. . . . Sellery may be eaten in Composition with other Sallet Herbs, or alone, with Oil, Vinegar, Salt, and Pepper." Celery was also chopped, cooked, and made into a delicate sauce.

The term *sallet* referred to a wide range of vegetable dishes eaten raw or cooked. For John Evelyn, the diarist and author of *Acetaria: A Discourse of Sallets,* a finely composed *sallet* was a symphony

> [in which] every Plant should come in to bear its part, without being over-power'd by some Herb of a stronger Taste, so as to endanger the native Sapor and vertue of the rest; but fall into their places, like the Notes in Music, in which there should be nothing harsh or grating: And tho' admitting some Discords (to distinguish and illustrate the rest) striking in the more sprightly, and sometimes gentler Notes, reconcile all Dissonancies, and melt them into an agreeable Composition.

FRUITS.   Native and "outlandish" (foreign) fruits were plentiful in England; there were over fifty varieties of pear alone, not to mention an abundance of quince, apples, plums, and wild berries. Kalm describes a clever method devised to bring Mediterranean fruits to quick ripening in English soil:

24

> Around most of the gardens here in England there were built brick-walls of various heights. . . . When anyone had a fruit tree which he wished to be able to bear either early or ripe fruit, the same was planted, if the wall ran from west to east, on the south side of, and close against the wall. . . . By reason of the tree thus coming to stand right in the heat of the sun, it could not be otherwise than that its fruit should be very early ripe and very beautiful. Apricots, Pistachios, Peaches, in their manifold varieties, with other beautiful fruits, were managed in the same way.

By this method, orange, lemon, and citron trees were occasionally made to fruit in England, but citrus was for the most part imported. In cookery the bitter Seville orange was preferred, but as the century progressed, the sweeter China orange increased in popularity both as an ingredient and for garniture.

Tomatoes were known but regarded with great suspicion; they never appear in recipes. Probably because they were recognized as members of the deadly nightshade family, tomatoes, often referred to as "love apples," were cultivated in gardens only as a curiosity and for the "amorous aspect of beauty of the fruit."[8]

The pineapple, on the other hand, was received with great delight when first brought to Britain from Barbados during Cromwell's era. English gardeners began to grow it early in the eighteenth century. For many years thereafter pineries were considered fashionable additions to those great estates that had their own hothouses, and wealthy hosts liked to offer their guests dishes which made use of homegrown pineapples (recipe, p. 148).

25

SALTING, PICKLING, AND CONDIMENTS. Many housewives were no doubt relieved to read in *The Country Housewife and Lady's Director* that "as for the common Notion, that Women cannot lay Meat in Salt, equally with success, at all Times, it is false; it is the Manner of doing it, and not the state of the Women who handle it, that makes it right." A mixture of salts was typically used for preserving, and alum was generally added to retain the color of food being pickled.

Sarah Harrison gives the following recipe for salting hams and tongues:

> Take three or four Gallons of Water, put to it two Ounces of Prunella Salt, four Pounds of white Salt, four Pounds of Bay Salt, a Quarter of a Pound of Salt-peter, an Ounce of Allum, a Pound of brown Sugar; let it boil a quarter of an Hour, scum it well; when it is cold, sever it from the Bottom into the Vessel you steep it in.
>
> Let Hams lie in this Pickle four or five Weeks, a Clod of Dutch Beef as long; Tongues a Fortnight; Collar'd Beef eight or ten Days. Dry them in a Stove or Wood Chimney.

The price of salt fluctuated but was frequently high, due to shortages of local supplies. Perhaps for this reason, cooks began relying on anchovies, capers, mustard (recipe, p. 124), and a variety of ketchups to bring out the taste of meats and sauces. Ketchup had become known through the East India Company's trade in China and Malaya, where a fish-and-brine pickle was used in flavoring foods. The idea of creating long-lasting liquid condiments gave rise to ketchups of anchovy, walnut, and mushroom, among others. These, of course, were ancestors of the bottled meat sauces so popular in England today.

Further evidence of an Eastern influence are the numerous recipes "To Make Mangoes," such as the one below, from Elizabeth Wainwright's manuscript cookbook. Because mango pickle was a favored import, the word mango became a generic label for a variety of pickles.

> Take Larg[e] Green Cowcumbers; pick out ye seeds & put in one Cowcumber, half a blade of Mace, 3 Cloves, a Lettel Peper, a Littel slic't genger, one Clove of Garlick, then fill it up wt horsradish: put the same sort of Spices in your Alegar & Scold ym 3 times—4 days betwixt scoldings. A bit of Alom in ye Alegar helps ym to green.

Most cookery books contain large sections on pickling such items as *broum buds* (the local caper), *hartechock bottoms, cockels, wallnuts,* mushrooms, and cabbages (recipe, p. 122). These were generally soaked for two to four weeks in a solution of vinegar (or *alegar*), mustard, and spices.

BREADS, BISCUITS, CAKES, AND CONFECTIONS. Breads were divided into three categories: white, wheaten, and household (mixed grain). By the early eighteenth century, most bread was purchased from the local baker, but widespread adulteration and short-weighting forced authorities to regulate the size and quality of loaves. According to the Assize of Bread enacted in 1710, any bread intended for sale had to be stamped in code letters which specified its contents and weight. The legal price of loaves fluctuated throughout the period and depended on the current price of wheat; thus the weight of a wheaten penny-loaf, called for in so many recipes, ranged from six to seven ounces. A white loaf weighed between four and five, and a household loaf about eight. Since the weight of the penny-loaf constantly shifted, but all of the recipes merely call for "a penny-loaf made into crumbs by rubbing in cloth," we can assume that the precise amount of crumbs used for thickening was left to the cook's better judgment.[9]

The term biscuit (from the French *bis cuit,* or twice cooked) was originally applied to those cakes which were first baked, then sliced and returned to the oven for drying. A particularly popular biscuit of this type was the Naples biscuit (recipe, p. 142), generally enriched with eggs and flavored with rose or orange-flower water. By the eighteenth century, the separate drying stage was often eliminated; instead, the biscuits were baked "in a slow Oven" until thoroughly dry. A most unusual biscuit of this type was the crimson biscuit (recipe, p. 140) made with the cooked pulp of beet and perfumed with orange-flower water. Puffs, little meringues flavored with either ground nuts, grated chocolate, or puréed fruit, were baked precisely the same way (recipe, p. 144).

At this time the word cake was used rather loosely, referring to the enriched, sweetened, yeasted seed cake (recipe, p. 156), the rolled, cookie-like Shrewsbury cake (recipe, p. 146), and even the little molded fruit and jelly pastes eaten as sweetmeats for dessert.

Fancy confections could be purchased in London shops, but most cookery books give ample space to directions for preparing them at home. Before the days of thermometers, the housewife had to recognize the various stages of boiling sugar for candy-making. One manuscript cookery book gives the following advice for recognizing sugar "When Boil'd to a Casting Height":

After ye Sugar is clarified Set it to boile againe till it is Somthing thicke, then Stir it wth a Sticke & Somtimes Swing your Stick from you & when it is boiled to a Casting height it will draw between your Fingers in great Flackes like Fethers or like great Flackes of Snow Flying in ye Ayre & So you may use it as you please.[10]

Mrs. Mary Eales, "Confectioner to her late Majesty Queen Anne," wrote a number of cookbooks devoted almost entirely to candy-making. A good many cookbooks of the period describe the preparation of fruit candies (recipe, p. 176), molded jellies, and candied peel (recipe, p. 103). Mrs. Eales recommends coloring these confections "red with carmine, yellow with gumboodge, brown with chocolate, and blue with smalt."

BEVERAGES. "Englishmen are great drinkers," writes yet another French visitor, César de Saussure. "In [their] coffeehouses you can partake of chocolate, tea, coffee, and of all sorts of liquors, served hot; also in many places you can have wine, punch, or ale."[11]

Of the non-alcoholic beverages, tea was the most favored among all classes of English society. It was so popular, in fact, that servants negotiated daily allotments of tea into their contracts, and belowstairs staff in wealthy households earned extra pennies by selling used tea leaves to the poor.

There were a few who considered tea (pronounced "tay") an unhealthy, tasteless drink which was glorified by the rich only because it came from an exotic land:

If China, or Japan, bore Hay,
And we had plenty of their Tea,
Growing amongst us in this Land,
The Ladies wou'd, no doubt command
That Cargoes shou'd be bought of Hay,
And spurn with pride their native Tea. . . .
If any Virtue we can find
In foreign Tea of any kind,
The Sugar works the powerful Cure,
And not the Tea, we may be sure. . . .
Tea cure the Megrim of the Head?
It rather helps to piss the Bed.

John Waldron, *A Satyr against Tea* (1733)

The general public turned a deaf ear to such invectives. In 1710, Thomas Twining set up his tea shop in the Strand, and a year later Queen Anne gave the drink the royal stamp of approval by appointing him her purveyor. All tea was imported from China; the best-quality green tea was called hyson, and the finest black, bohea. By the end of the century, over twenty million pounds were imported annually.

Many cookbooks of the period contain an ample chapter on distilling, and if the following sketch from the contemporary play *Adam and Eve Stript' of their Furbelows* is to be believed, the household stillroom must have been quite a "spirited" place.

It would make a Man smile to behold her Figure in a front Box, where her twinkling eyes, by her Afternoon's Drams of Ratifee and cold Tea, sparkle more than her Pendants. . . . Her Closet is always as well stor'd with Juleps, Restoratives, and Strong Waters, as an Apothecary's Shop, or a Distiller's Laboratory; and is herself so notable a Housewife in the Art of preparing them that she has a larger Collection of Chemical Receipts than a Dutch Mountebank. . . .

Cordials were usually named for their primary flavoring agent, and types were as numerous as their names were charming: Ratafia of Apricocks, Millefleurs, Orangiat, Burgamot, to list just a few.

But the staple spirit of the age was gin, and no tax or legislation could effectively stop its flow. In England alone, there were two million gallons distilled in 1714, eleven million in 1733, and twenty million in 1742.[12] One has only to think of Hogarth's *Gin Lane* to picture the devastating effect this drink had on the London poor.

Besides gin, French and Portuguese (port) wines, and homemade cordials, the English drank corn spirits from Holland and rum and arrack from the West Indies. The latter were frequently used to make punch (recipe, p. 186), a popular drink available at most of London's five-hundred-odd coffeehouses. Kalm relates the following story, which painfully reveals the English devotion to this beverage despite experience with its adverse effects:

I asked Mr. Catesby and Dr. Mitchel whether they thought that Punch was a useful or a baneful drink. They answered that their opinion was that it is beneficial or baneful according as it is prepared. . . . They drank at one time Punch which was made of strong Brandywine or rum and water with much sugar in it, but only a little lemon-juice was added. The effect, which they gradually found, of this was, that after some time they got a kind of Paralysis, which was such that they could not hold anything with the fingers. . . .

Afterwards they began to diminish the quantity of Brandywine and sugar but to put more lemon-juice in it, after which they did not get such troublesome paralysis, although commonly the sad future consequence was that he who drank Punch generally became very palsied in his old age.

Eating Out

In the eighteenth century, the traveler had difficulty finding a decent meal along the road. Inn food was, generally speaking, intolerable. Fielding puts the matter quite succinctly:

> We must . . . attend Mr. Jones to Mrs. Water's Apartment, where the Dinner which he had now bespoke was on the Table. Indeed it took no long Time in preparing, having been all drest three Days before, and required nothing more from the Cook than to warm it over again. (386)

In 1732, one fourth of all houses in London were involved with the selling of food or drink, and one could eat fairly well at a tavern, restaurant, or cook's shop.[13] Many taverns and chophouses had their own specialties: *calipash* and *calipee* at the King's Arms, beefsteaks at Dolly's. It was often the custom for the diner to enter the kitchen and select the steak of his choice from among those being broiled over the coals.

Pontack's was considered the finest "ordinary" of the time, but there were other restaurants that vied for first place by offering sophisticated French-style food. In the words of Ned Ward:

> At Locket's, Brown's and at Pontack's enquire,
> What modish Kick shaws the nice Beaus desire,
> What famed Ragoust, what new invented Salate
> Has best pretentions to regale the Palate.[14]

For a quick meal at good value for the money, one went to a cook's shop. Misson describes four spits at work simultaneously within, each rotating five or six pieces of meat: beef, mutton, veal, pork, and lamb. "You have what Quantity you please cut off, fat, lean, much or little done; with this, a little Salt and Mustard upon the Side of a Plate, a Bottle of Beer, and a Roll; and there is your whole Feast."

From May through September, the London pleasure gardens—Ranelagh and Vauxhall being the most famous—opened their gates to concertgoers, social dancers, and those who wished a cooling stroll beneath the trees. According to *The Connoisseur* (May 15, 1755), eating was a vital necessity for visitors to the gardens: "We dare not lay ourselves on the damp ground in shady groves or by the purling stream [unless at least] we fortify our insides against the cold by good substantial eating and drinking."

At Ranelagh, it was fashionable to hear the morning concert in the giant rotunda while breakfasting on bread and butter with coffee or tea. At Vauxhall, evening attendance was preferred, and those who dined in the supper boxes after the concert chose from a selection of cold meats, salads, cheeses, cakes, and wines listed on the "Bill of Provisions." If we are to believe the following letter written by Horace Walpole in 1750, some merrymakers found it amusing to cook dinner on the spot.

> [Lady Caroline Petersham] had fetched my brother Orford from the next box, where he was enjoying himself with his *petite partie,* to help us to mince chickens. We minced seven chickens into a china dish, which Lady Caroline stewed over a lamp, with three pats of butter and a flagon of water, stirring and rattling and laughing, and we every minute expecting the dish to fly about our ears. . . . In short the whole air of our party was sufficient . . . to take up the whole attention of the Gardens. . . . It was three o'clock before we got home.

Gentlemen frequently ate at their clubs. Since clubs were generally founded on the basis of strong political as well as gastronomic allegiances, their names and menus were often rich in symbolic import. For example, at the Calves' Head Club, established to ridicule the memory of Charles I,

> their bill of fare was a large dish of calves' heads, dressed several ways, by which they represented the king and his friends who had suffered in his cause; a large pike, with a small one in his mouth, as an emblem of tyranny; a large cod's head, by which they intended to represent the person of the king singly; a boar's head with an apple in its mouth, to represent the king by this as bestial, as by their other hieroglyphics they had done foolish and tyrannical.[15]

It was traditional in some clubs for members to present gifts of food in lieu of dues; thus on May 3, 1750, the Royal Society Club announced: "Resolved, that any nobleman or gentleman complimenting this company annually with venison, not less than a haunch, shall, during the continuance of such annuity, be deemed an Honorary Member." Later that year, it was suggested that turtle would be a valid gift, and on one occasion, so the club's records report, the usual kitchen could not be used, since the West Indian turtle imported for that day's dinner weighed four hundred pounds.

Eating at Home

THE GEORGIAN KITCHEN. In a sprawling eighteenth-century country house, the kitchen, pantry, and scullery were either located in one wing or existed as a freestanding stone or brick structure attached to the main house by a covered passageway. The object in both cases was to keep cooking odors and smoke as far away from the family living quarters as possible.

Judging by Rowlandson's drawing *The Squire's Kitchen,* the room was of considerable size and doubled as the servants' dining room. A large fireplace was built into the center of one wall, and a chimney crane attached to its inside wall held pots that could be swung to rest over the fire.

In the fireplace, spits were notched into position like rungs of a wide iron ladder. A dripping pan was set below them to catch the fats and juices of roasting meats. Spits were turned manually or, more typically, by a variety of elaborate contrivances: dogs running inside a wheel attached by chains to the spits; smoke jacks operated by the hot air rising in the chimney; gravity spits pulled around by cords with heavy weights attached to their ends. Large hunks of meat were sometimes hooked onto dangle spits which hung vertically and revolved back and forth at the whim of a wind-up mechanism.

Large cauldrons, hanging or three-legged, were generally made of brass or cast iron, but Mrs. Glasse warns in *The Art of Cookery* that "iron is not proper," reflecting a fear that lead poisoning might be contracted from badly made vessels. Smaller pots, called pipkins, were often made of copper, but there was cause for concern if they were not tin-lined. In a pamphlet entitled *Serious Reflections Attending the Use of Copper Vessels* (1755), the author states that "the great frequency of palsies, apoplexies, madness, and all frightful train of nervous disorders . . . are the pernicious effects of this poisonous matter taken into the body insensibly with our vittles."[16]

Gridirons, used for broiling or grilling meat and fish, were either held manually over the fire or rested on round iron frames called brandreths. "When grilling," states the author of *The Whole Duty of a Woman,* "let it be over a stove of Charcoal, rather than Sea Coal; it makes it eat sweeter and shorter; turn your meat very often."

Among the smaller implements in the kitchen were iron bread toasters, made with either hooks or grates. Chestnut roasters, perforated cylindrical iron boxes attached to long handles, came into popular use, as did the coffee roaster, similar in design, created to roast the "berries" for that popular drink. Kettles, boot-shaped ale-warmers, wafering irons, warming pans, salamanders, skimmers, sugar nippers, pastry jiggers—all these were available to the eighteenth-century cook.

This is not to say that life in the often smoky kitchen was easy. No major work-saving

Thomas Rowlandson, *The Squire's Kitchen*

device had yet been invented, and it was not until late in the century that Rumford and Robinson began developing a kitchen range. The cook's lot was difficult, and judging by Swift's ironic "Directions to the Cook," this member of the household was often neither pleased nor pleasing:

> If a lump of soot falls into the soup, and you cannot conveniently get it out, scum it well, and it will give the soup a high French taste.

> Never clean your spits after they have been used; for the grease left upon them by meat, is the best thing to preserve them from rust; and when you make use of them again, the same grease will keep the inside of the meat moist.

> When you find that you cannot get dinner ready at the time appointed, put the clock back, and then it may be ready to a minute.[17]

MEALTIMES.   Those comfortably off normally ate three meals a day: breakfast about ten, dinner any time from two until seven, and supper about nine. The hours varied from one household to another and were in a constant state of flux throughout the century.

For the fashionable, it was late-to-bed and late-to-rise, and it was not unusual for the likes of decadent Lady Bellaston to take breakfast in bed "very late in the Morning." Breakfast was usually a "dish" of tea (with milk and sugar) accompanied by toasted bread, but some ladies found it necessary first to stimulate their appetites with hot chocolate:

> Wednesday from Eight 'till Ten. Drank two Dishes of Chocolate in Bed, and fell asleep after 'em.

> From Ten to Eleven. Ate a Slice of Bread and Butter, drank a dish of Bohea,
> read *The Spectator*.[18]

The more industrious spent the hours between rising and breakfast by reading, walking, writing letters, or, in the case of the young law student Dudley Ryder, darning socks. Ryder sometimes substituted birch wine for tea, while gluttonous Squire Western, in his inimitably thirsty way, washed down his buttered toast with a "Tankard."[19]

Taking a snack a few hours after breakfast was a popular habit. Around midday, gentlemen frequently stopped at their favorite coffeehouses to read the morning newspaper while sipping a drink. This noontime refreshment was called nunch (noon + Old English *scenc,* or cup) and sometimes included a small pie or some biscuits to stave off hunger.[20]

The main meal, dinner, was eaten later and later in the day as the century progressed. "In my memory," wrote Richard Steele in *The Tatler* (1710), "the dinner hour has crept from twelve o'clock to three." By the 1740s many ate even later:

> The Shadows began now to descend larger from the high Mountains: The feather'd Creation had betaken themselves to their Rest. Now the highest Order of Mortals were sitting down to their Dinners, and the lowest Order to their Suppers. In a Word, the Clock struck five just as Mr. Jones took his Leave of Gloucester. . . . (331)

"Their Supper is moderate: Gluttons at noon, and abstinent at Night," comments Misson. Supper was generally a light meal of cold roasted meat and cheese. It was not unusual to skip this meal altogether, as does the distraught Sophia Western the evening she learns that Tom Jones shares her father's love of wenching.

THE CHINA MADNESS.

> "My sister," Lady Elizabeth Finch tells the Countess of Burlington in 1735, "is become China Mad, frequents all the shops in town in order to get either old or Dresden China, the first purchases she made of that sort of Ware were yellow & green tea Cups variously and most hideously intermingled as like Delf as ever was seen, but They told her 'twas old China and that was inducement enough to her to buy 'em however they are now exchang'd for a sett of Dresden."[21]

By the late seventeenth century, the fashionable English hostess was using plates and tea services imported from China. After 1709, when the process of making hard-paste porcelain was discovered at Meissen (near Dresden in Saxony), it gradually became stylish for the "lady of quality" to adorn her dining and tea tables with the more costly Dresden ware. Chinese porcelain still remained popular for everyday use, especially among those of more restricted means; a squire like Allworthy may well have owned a service for twenty, hand-painted with his armorial shield.

Ladies found amusement in ambling from one London china shop to the next, comparing wares and prices, much to the vexation of the shopkeepers:

> One of these No Customers, calls for a Set of Tea Dishes, another for a Bason, a third for my best Green Tea, and even to the Punchbowl; there's scarce a piece in my Shop but must be displaced, and the whole agreeable Architecture disordered.
>
> . . . Well, after all this Racket and Clutter, this is too dear, that is their

Aversion; another thing is Charming, but not wanted. The Ladies are cured of the Spleen, but I am not a Shilling the better for it.[22]

"Serve it in a China dish," instruct scores of recipes. Apparently the ladies did, at last, make their purchases.

DINNER: LAYING THE TABLE AND SERVING THE MEAL.   "An Englishman's table is remarkably clean, the linen is very white, the plate shines brightly, and knives and forks are changed surprisingly often, that is to say, every time a plate is removed," observes Saussure. For each course, the dinner guest was provided a "cover" consisting of a plate (silver or porcelain), fork, knife, spoon, napkin, and wine glass.

The fork in general use at the beginning of the century had only two widely separated prongs and was therefore impractical for eating small morsels. Yet the "modern" three-pronged affair was still fighting something of a battle for acceptance:

> As late as 1729 the poet Gay begs Swift, when the latter is invited to stay with the Duchess of Queensberry, not to eat with the point of his knife, nor to despise a fork with three prongs. Swift replies in self-justification that at a poor house forks were only bi-dental, that at Mr. Pope's it was impossible, without a knife, to convey a morsel of beef with the incumbrance of mustard and turnips into your mouth.[23]

Most knives at this time were made with broad ends, and the English were renowned for their skill in balancing peas and the juice of fruit pies on the tips.

Finely embroidered damask napkins were often folded decoratively into the shapes of animals, flowers, or birds. Samuel Pepys noted in his *Diary,* late in the seventeenth century, that he was "mightily pleased with the fellow that came to lay the cloth and fold the napkins; which I like so well as that I am resolved to give him forty shillings to teach my wife to do it."

Many cookbooks of the period have elaborate diagrams instructing the hostess and her servants how to present food properly. These plans for setting out the platters were called ambigues, and they were often so elaborate that foldout pages fifteen inches long were used to demonstrate the laying of a banquet table at a glance.[24] The arrangements were as symmetrical as a Handel sonata and reflect the age's notion that order was a sign of gentility.

In a manuscript cookery book dated c. 1700 by the British Library, Daniel Moult used his compass to record a typical dinner menu for a day in the late spring. His plan for first and second courses is reproduced on pages 44 and 45.

Although it was the function of servants to lay the table and stand by to remove the dishes as each course was completed, it was not customary for them to serve the food. The lady of the house did the "Honours of the Table" from her position at the head. Her first task was to spoon the soup from a large tureen into individual bowls which were passed along to the guests. As soon as the serving bowl was empty, it was removed and a large platter of meat or fish was put in its place. Diagrams indicated this intention by the wording: "A Carrot Soop remove Harrico of Mutton."

After the soup was eaten and the bowls cleared away, the mistress set about carving the roasted meat and arranging the slices on serving platters. Thus Mrs. Western "scarce indeed ever saw [Squire Western] but at Meals; where she had the Pleasure of carving those Dishes which she had before attended at the Dressing." Mrs. Western no doubt acquired her skill from the chapters on carving that could be found in almost every cookbook. They instruct: "Thigh that Woodcock. Lift that Swan. Rear that Goose. Tame that Crab."[25]

During the two main courses of the meal, guests were expected to help themselves from all of the platters arranged in the center of the table. Clearly, this custom invited the dilemma of the "boardinghouse reach." Since tables were large and each dish was not necessarily repeated on both sides, it took some complicated maneuvering to fill one's plate with a selection of the food being offered.

To overcome such difficulty, R. Bradley suggested in *The Country Housewife and Lady's Director* that all platters be placed on a round tray which was one foot less in diameter than the table; this "lazy Susan" could easily be spun around on top of a four-inch-high brass spindle so that "in its turning about, no Salt, or Bread, or anything on the Plates, may be disturb'd. It remains then for the Lady of the House, to offer the Soop; but after that, every one is at Liberty to help themselves, by turning the upper Table about." Bradley's invention was recommended by numerous cookbook authors as a practical way to serve food while still abiding by the laws of fashion.

First Course

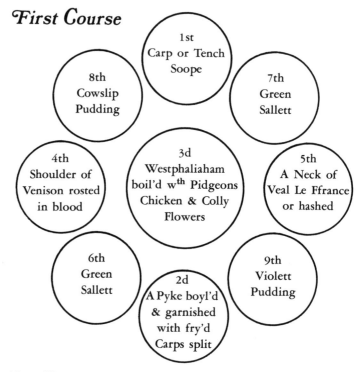

1st
Carp or Tench
Soope

8th
Cowslip
Pudding

7th
Green
Sallett

4th
Shoulder of
Venison rosted
in blood

3d
Westphaliaham
boil'd wth Pidgeons
Chicken & Colly
Flowers

5th
A Neck of
Veal Le Ffrance
or hashed

6th
Green
Sallett

2d
A Pyke boyl'd
& garnished
with fry'd
Carps split

9th
Violett
Pudding

The middle Dish in first & second Course are to be plac'd upon a stand 4 inches high & the 4 small Dishes in both Courses are to be placed upon 4 Rings 2 inches high each the rest of the Dishes to stand flat upon the Table.

44

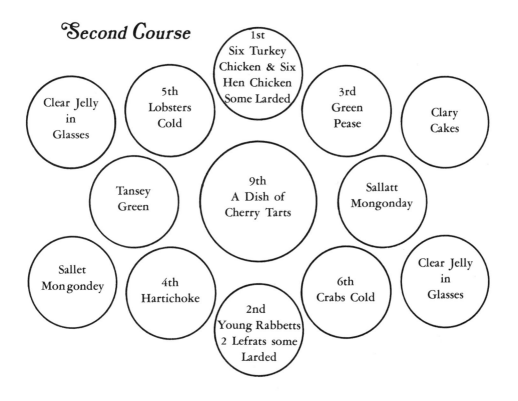

Second Course

1st
Six Turkey
Chicken & Six
Hen Chicken
Some Larded

3rd
Green
Pease

Clary
Cakes

Clear Jelly
in
Glasses

5th
Lobsters
Cold

Tansey
Green

9th
A Dish of
Cherry Tarts

Sallatt
Mongonday

Sallet
Mongondey

4th
Hartichoke

2nd
Young Rabbetts
2 Lefrats some
Larded

6th
Crabs Cold

Clear Jelly
in
Glasses

DESSERT AND TOASTS. When dinner was done, the table was cleared and the cloth removed or swept clean of crumbs. Guests were provided small plates, silverware, and glasses, and dessert was brought on if it had not already been present as part of the arrangement of the second course.

Dessert provided hostess and cook the opportunity to let all creative energies come to the fore. Massiolot, in *The Court and Country Cook*, gives two methods for "dressing" dessert: "In a Basket" and "On the Level." According to instructions for the former, each guest at "certain Fraternity" dinners was to receive a small earthenware basket adorned with "small Ribbands, and Taffety-covers," and filled with dry sweetmeats such as candied orange peel, fruit pastes, and marzipan. The basket was given as a favor and meant to be taken home intact. At the dinner itself, guests could content themselves with the slices of cheese, jellies, fools, creams, and ices arranged attractively in the center of the table.

"On the Level" was the more typical way to end meals. In Squire Allworthy's house, such a dessert might have consisted of a display of molded jellies surrounding a potted Cheshire cheese (recipe, p. 180), or a large dish of assorted preserved fruits piled high on a tall silver salver and set off with fresh leaves.

Dessert arrangements became more elaborate as the century wore on, and Lady Bellaston, with the help of her cooks and servants, might have offered a dessert course something like this:

Ice cream, different colors.

Clear jellies
in glasses.

Whip'd syllabubs.

Lemon cream
in glasses.

In the middle a
high pyramid
of one salver
above another,
the bottom one
large, the next
smaller, the
top one less;
these salvers
are to be fill'd
with all kinds
of wet and dry
sweet-meats
in glass, baskets
or little plates,
colour'd jellies,
creams, &c.
biscuits, crisp'd
almonds and
little knicknacks,
and bottles of
flowers prettily
intermix'd, the
little top salver
must have a large
preserv'd Fruit
in it.

Nonpareils.

Golden
pippins.

Bloomage stuck
with almonds.

Bloomage stuck
with almonds.

Postalia nuts.

Almonds
and raisins.

Lemon cream
in glasses.

Whip'd syllabubs.

Clear jellies
in glasses.

Ice cream, different colors.[26]

Plans even more elaborate than the one above call for inedible ornaments representing "gravel walks, hedges . . . and a little Chinese Temple in the middle," or a "large dish with figures and grass or moss about it and flowers only for shew." So flamboyant were some of the artificial centerpieces that Horace Walpole satirized them in his *Fugitive Pieces* (1753):

> Jellies, biscuits, sugar-plumbs and creams have long given way to harlequins, gondoliers, Turks, Chinese, and shepherdesses of Saxon China. But these, unconnected, and only seeming to wander among groves of curled paper and silk flowers, were soon discovered to be too insipid and unmeaning. By degrees whole meadows of cattle, of the same brittle materials, spread themselves over the whole table; cottages rose in sugar, and temples in barley-sugar; pigmy Neptunes in cars of cockle-shells triumphed over oceans of looking-glass. . . . Confectioners found their trade moulder away, while toymen and china shops were the only fashionable purveyors of the last stage of polite entertainments.

After dessert, it was the custom to sit "for an hour at the table," reports Kalm, "or at least as long as till certain toasts have been drunk by all, such as the King's health, the Prince of Wales, the Royal Family, absent friends, &c." Saussure is astonished that "after these toasts the women rise and leave the room, the men paying them no attention or asking them to stay; the men remain together for a longer or lesser time. This custom surprises foreigners, especially Frenchmen, who are infinitely more polite with regard to women than are Englishmen; but it is the custom and one must submit."[27] So customary is this behavior, that even after her wedding-day dinner Sophia takes "the first Opportunity of withdrawing with the Ladies," leaving Squire Western "to his Cups."

Eventually the women were joined by the men in the drawing room, where they converged around the tea table for a "dish of Bohea," lively conversation, and perhaps a game of whist.

Notes to the Introduction

1. Lord Ernle, *English Farming Past and Present*. 6th ed. (Chicago, 1961), p. 148ff. The chapters "Jethro Tull and Lord Townshend: 1700–1760" and "The Stock-breeder's Art and Robert Bakewell: 1725–1795" are particularly relevant. The high standard of living is accountable in part to Townshend's invention of a system of crop rotation which made available large quantities of turnips; these were used as cheap winter fodder for cattle, and for the first time, large quantities of meat were available to English people all year round.

2. J. E. Zetzner, *Londres et Angleterre, A.D. 1700.* Quoted in Rosamund Bayne-Powell, *Travellers in Eighteenth-Century England* (London, 1951), p. 47.

3. Peter Kalm, *Kalm's Visit to England: 1748,* translated by Joseph Lucas (London, 1892), p. 15. Page numbers of subsequent quotations from Kalm may be found by consulting the index to this text.

4. Henry Fielding, *Tom Jones,* edited by Sheridan Baker (New York, 1973), p. 141. Page numbers of subsequent quotations of substantial length will be indicated in parentheses and refer to this text.

5. M. Misson, *M. Misson's Memoirs and Observations,* translated by Ozell (London, 1919), p. 315. Page numbers of subsequent quotations from Misson may be found by consulting the index to this text.

6. G. Eland, editor, *Purefoy Letters,* vol. 1 (London, 1931), p. 62.

7. Daniel Defoe, *A Tour thro' Great Britain,* vol. 1 (London, 1748), p. 65.

8. See C. Anne Wilson, *Food and Drink in Britain* (London, 1973), p. 320 ff. Numerous details of interest mentioned throughout the Introduction were first encountered here.

9. I am grateful to Elizabeth David, who pointed this out to me in private correspondence.

10. Dennis Rhodes, editor, *In an Eighteenth Century Kitchen* (London, 1968), p. 8.

11. César de Saussure, *A Foreign View of England in the Reigns of George I and George II,* translated and edited by Madame Van Muyden (New York, 1902), p. 221. Page numbers of subsequent quotations from Saussure may be found by consulting the index to this text.

12. André Simon, *Bottlescrew Days* (London, 1926), p. 22.

13. Dorothy Davis, *Fairs, Shops, and Supermarkets: A History of English Shopping* (Toronto, 1966), p. 189. The author gives her source as W. Maitland, *History and Survey of London* (1756).

14. Quoted in John Ashton, *Social Life in the Reign of Queen Anne* (London, 1904), p. 142.

15. John Timbs, *Clubs and Club Life in London* (Detroit, 1967), p. 1. Subsequent material on clubs is taken from this volume.

16. Quoted in J. Seymour Lindsay, *Iron and Brass Implements of the English House* (London, 1970), p. 27. Fireplace and cooking equipment from early history through the nineteenth century are carefully illustrated in this volume. For related material, see Molly Harrison, *The Kitchen in History* (Reading, 1972); Dorothy Hartley, *Food in England* (London, 1975); Mary Norwak, *Kitchen Antiques* (London, 1975); Lawrence Wright, *Home Fires Burning* (London, 1964).

17. Jonathan Swift, *Directions to Servants* (New York, 1964), pp. 51–62. In this "treatise," Swift also gives directions to the butler, house steward, and dairymaid, among others.

18. *The Spectator*, edited by Donald F. Bond, vol. 3 (Oxford, 1965), p. 182.

19. Dudley Ryder, *The Diary of Dudley Ryder*, edited by William Matthews (London, 1939), passim. The Virginia gentleman William Byrd began almost every day of his four-year sojourn in London with nothing but a dish of boiled milk. See William Byrd of Virginia, *The London Diary . . .* (New York, 1958), passim.

20. More ravenous laboring folk took a midday meal called lunch (from lump, as in lump of cheese). Dr. Johnson, in his *Dictionary* (1755), defines nuncheon as a "piece of victuals eaten between meals," while luncheon is "as much food as one's hand can hold." Johnson derived the latter definition from his mistaken notion that the word lunch was etymologically related to "clutch."

21. Quoted in Elizabeth Burton, *The Georgians at Home* (London, 1973), p. 156. The letter is dated May 29, 1735, and is catalogued Chatsworth MSS 230-5.

22. *The Spectator*, op. cit., vol. 4, p. 479.

23. Quoted in Rose Bradley, *The English Housewife in the Seventeenth and Eighteenth Centuries* (London, 1912), p. 106. Unfortunately, no source is given.

24. The word ambigue is derived from French and is related to our word ambiguous (i.e., that which seems to have more than one identity). The *Oxford English Dictionary* gives a contemporary (1753) definition: "Ambigu denotes a kind of mixed entertainment, wherein both flesh and fruit are served together." In many of the table plans, preserved fruits and sweetmeats form the centerpiece for the second meat course. For the most elaborate ambigues, see Charles Carter, *The Compleat City and Country Cook: or, Accomplished Housewife*, 3rd ed., 1732.

25. That some amount of carving was left to the individual guests is evident in a letter from Lord Chesterfield to his son:

    Since I am upon little things, I must mention another, which, though little enough in itself, yet, as it occurs at least once in every day, deserves some attention: I mean Carving. Do you use yourself to carve adroitly and genteely; without hacking half an hour across a bone; without bespattering the company with the sauce; and without overturning the glasses into your neighbour's pockets?

See Lord Chesterfield, *Letters written by Earl of Chesterfield to his Son, Philip Stanhope,* edited by Mrs. Eugenia Stanhope, vol. 2 (London, 1800), p. 104 and passim.

26. Hannah Glasse, *The Compleat Confectioner* (Dublin, 1762), p. 263.

27. Professor James Clifford has an interesting theory to explain this behavior:

> I have often wondered whether the major reason for the separation of males and females after dinner—so accepted as part of social behaviours in the eighteenth century, and today as well—originated from physical necessity. There were no bathrooms, and the men relieved themselves in the dining room, pots being readily available from the sideboards, while the ladies went off to commodes in other parts of the house. . . . The Duc de la Rochefoucauld, in describing one dinner he attended in London, commented: "The sideboard too is furnished with a number of chamber pots and it is a common practice to relieve oneself whilst the rest are drinking; one has no kind of concealment and the practice strikes me as most indecent."

See James Clifford, "Some Aspects of London Life in the Mid-18th Century," *City and Society in the Eighteenth Century,* edited by Paul Fritz and David Williams (Toronto, 1973), p. 29.

On Preparing the Recipes

In choosing the sixty-odd recipes for this volume, I followed the goals set forth by Eliza Smith in her preface to *The Compleat Housewife,* including only those "wholesome, toothsome, . . . practicable and easy to be performed." Most of the dishes that follow may be found, perhaps slightly altered, in a good number of the cookbooks of the period, and many of them can be traced back to earlier times.

I spent some very happy hours in libraries, pouring over the old cookbooks, conjuring up tastes suggested by the recipes, and silently smacking my lips. Once back in the kitchen, I found the recipes great fun to prepare and as delicious to eat as I had imagined. The ingredients were familiar enough to invite a sense of comfort, yet combinations and methods of preparation were often exciting and new. For example, you'll be needing a pudding cloth; any clean piece of cotton or tightly woven linen fabric about fifteen inches square will do. Then you'll want to stock up on such items as sweet butter, anchovies, capers, orange-flower water, and rose water.

A few more suggestions might be in order:

—Establish a warm and friendly relationship with your butcher. That way he'll be more inclined to answer your questions and honor unusual requests.

—Use a potato peeler with a light but firm stroke to cut the peel from oranges and lemons. With a very sharp knife, shave off any white pith from the inside of the peel.

—Freeze egg whites in individual ice-cube containers. Pop them out and store the frozen cubes in a large plastic bag until needed.

—Freeze gravy (recipe, p. 132) in the same way, making sure to measure a full $\frac{1}{4}$ cup into each cube. Small amounts of gravy are used in many of the recipes; defrost as needed.

The original recipes are offered intact, including irregularities of spelling and capitalization. Selections from the manuscript cookery books often use abbreviations such as "ym" for them, and "wt" for with; these have been maintained as well. All archaic and unusual terms are defined in the Glossary.

In my adaptations I have generally remained faithful to the proportions suggested in the originals, and have called the reader's attention to significant deviations. Concluding as I began, with the words of Eliza Smith: "[I have confidence that] these Receipts . . . if rightly observed, will prevent the spoiling of many a good Dish of Meat, the Waste of many good Materials, the Vexation that frequently attends such Mismanagements, and the Curses not unfrequently bestowed on Cooks, with the usual Reflection, that whereas God sends good Meat, the Devil sends Cooks."

Bon Appétit

OF SOOPS, POTTAGES, AND A NUMBER OF PRETTY LITTLE DISHES

An Almond Soop

Take a Quart of Almonds, blanch them, and beat them in a Marbel Mortar, with the Yolks of twelve hard Eggs, till they are a fine Paste; mix by degrees with two Quarts of New Milk, a Quart of Cream, a Quarter of a Pound of double-refin'd-Sugar beat fine, a Pennyworth of Orange flower water, stir all well together; when it is well mixed, set it over a slow Fire, keep it stirring quick all the while, till you find it thick enough, then pour it into your Dish, and send it to the Table. If you don't be very careful it will curdle.

Hannah Glasse, *The Art of Cookery*

Almond Soup. In English cuisine, the sweet Jordan almond (from the French *jardin,* or garden) was used more than the bitter variety, but the latter enjoyed a certain popularity during the eighteenth century for flavoring ratafia puffs (recipe, p. 144), cordials, and creams. Bitter almonds have been found to contain a toxic substance, and are no longer available for purchase.

The almond milk of the Middle Ages, an infusion of ground almonds and sweetened broth or wine, was an important substitute for cow's milk on fasting days. As the religious need for this dish diminished, the recipe evolved over the years to a rich soup with a milk-and-cream base and an echo of orange-flower water. In warm weather, you may wish to serve it chilled. Plan on small portions; *almond soop* is very rich.

1 cup (scant $\frac{1}{2}$ pound) blanched almonds
yolks of 3 hard-boiled eggs
2 cups milk
1 cup heavy cream
1 tablespoon sugar
$\frac{1}{2}$ teaspoon (or more) orange-flower water

1. Grind almonds and egg yolks in a blender, or pound them to a paste with a mortar and pestle.
2. In a soup pot, combine ground almonds and egg yolks with remaining ingredients.
3. Heat but do not boil, stirring until well blended. Check seasoning.
4. Serve in teacups or small bowls.

SERVES 6

To Make Onion Soop

Take four or five large Onions, pill and boil them in Milk and Water whilst tender (shifting them two or three times in the boiling), beat them in a Marble Mortar to a Pulp, and rub them through a Hair Sieve, and put them into a little Sweet Gravy; then fry a few Slices of Veal, and two or three Slices of lean Bacon; beat them in a Marble Mortar as small as forc'd Meat; put it into your Stew-pan with the Gravy and Onions, and boil them; mix a Spoonful of wheat-flower with a little Water, and put it into the Soop to keep it from running: strain all through a Cullander, season it to your Taste; then put into the Dish a little Spinage stew'd in Butter, and a little crisp Bread; so serve it up.

Elizabeth Moxon, *English Housewifery*

Onion Soup. The word soup is related etymologically to sop, the toasted or fried bread it was often served with, as in the recipe below. This smooth, delicate soup is provided interesting contrasts in color and texture by the addition of spinach and "a little crisp Bread."

5 large onions (about 2 pounds), peeled and sliced

1 cup milk

3 slices lean bacon

$\frac{1}{4}$ pound veal (stewing quality), diced

oil

2 cups gravy (recipe, p. 132) or strong beef broth

salt and freshly ground pepper

2 tablespoons butter

$\frac{1}{2}$ pound spinach, washed, trimmed, and shredded

1 cup fried or toasted bread cubes

1. In a large soup pot, place onions, milk, and enough water to cover. Bring to a boil.
2. Cover and cook over medium heat about 20 minutes, or until onions are soft. Stir occasionally.
3. Drain onions. Reserve cooking liquid for another use; it makes a tasty soup base.
4. In a skillet, fry bacon and then veal, using a small amount of oil if needed. Drain.
5. In a blender, purée onions, bacon, and veal.
6. Pass purée and gravy through a fine-meshed strainer into soup pot.
7. Simmer, adding salt and pepper to taste.
8. Meanwhile, in a saucepan, melt butter. Add spinach. Cover and cook over medium heat, stirring once or twice, until wilted.
9. Place spinach and bread cubes in soup bowls. Pour soup over them. Serve hot.

    NOTE: I found this soup to be sufficiently thick without adding the "Spoonful of wheat-flower" suggested in the original recipe.

SERVES 4

To Make a Carrot-Soop

Boil your Carrots, cleanse them, beat them in a Mortar or Wooden Tray, put them into a Pipkin with Butter, White-wine, Salt, Cinnamon, Sugar, slic'd Dates, boil'd Currants, stew these well together, dish them on Sippets, garnish with hard Eggs in halves or quarters, and scrape on Sugar.

John Nott, *The Cook's and Confectioner's Dictionary*

Carrot Soup. The elevated status of root vegetables in eighteenth-century England is demonstrated by this unusual recipe. Try preparing the soup with baby carrots, as they are particularly flavorful.

2 pounds carrots, scrubbed, trimmed, and coarsely chopped
2 tablespoons butter

1 cup white wine
2 cups chicken broth*
$\frac{1}{4}$ teaspoon cinnamon
1 teaspoon sugar
salt
$\frac{1}{3}$ cup currants
$\frac{1}{2}$ cup dates, sliced and pitted
1 cup fried or toasted bread cubes
garnish: 2 large hard-boiled eggs, quartered or coarsely chopped
additional sugar

1. In a large soup pot, bring 3 quarts water to a rolling boil.
2. Cook carrots, covered, about 10 minutes, or until they can be easily pierced with a fork. Drain.
3. Purée carrots in a food mill or blender.
4. Place carrot purée in soup pot.
5. Stir in remaining ingredients except bread cubes, eggs, and additional sugar.
6. Bring to a boil, then simmer, uncovered, for 15 minutes.
7. Place bread cubes in soup bowls. Pour soup over them.
8. Garnish with hard-boiled eggs and dust lightly with additional sugar before serving.

SERVES 4–6

*Since the original recipe calls for wine as the sole liquid ingredient, you may prefer to use wine instead of chicken broth. For optimum flavor, use a good-quality wine.

Pease Pottage

Take 8 Pints of Pease, and 6 quarts of Water; set them on the Fire together with a large Onion, season them high, let them boil; and when they are enough, strain them through a Cullander, and set them on the Fire again; and when they are boiled, put in 4 handfuls of Spinage, two Leeks, a little Mint, 2 spoonfuls of Flour tempered with Water; then put in your Forc'd meat-balls, and a little after a pound of sweet butter; keep it stirring till the butter is melted; then dish it to the Table; don't cut the Herbs small, but gross; take care they don't lose their Colour; serve it.

Henry Howard, *England's Newest Way in All Sorts of Cookery*

Kitchen-Garden Pea Soup

Pease pottage hot, pease pottage cold,
Pease pottage in a pot, nine days old.

Not this one. It will be gone by the time you serve the entrée, and is actually hearty enough for lunch or a light supper on its own. Without the forcemeat balls, it is delicious cold.

4 cups chicken stock
3/4 teaspoon salt
3 cups shelled peas (3 pounds in pods)
1 small onion, peeled and chopped
1 leek, white part only, chopped
optional: 10–12 forcemeat balls (recipe, p. 82)
beurre manié: 1 tablespoon flour blended into 2 tablespoons butter
2 cups spinach, washed, trimmed, and coarsely shredded
1 tablespoon chopped fresh mint or 1 teaspoon dried
salt and freshly ground pepper
garnish: coarsely chopped fresh mint

1. In a large pot, bring stock and salt to a rolling boil.
2. Add peas and onion. Cook over medium heat about 15 minutes, or until peas are soft.
3. Place contents of pot in a blender and purée.
4. Return purée to pot.
5. Add leek and forcemeat balls (if you are using them). Cover and cook over low heat about 12 minutes, or until meatballs are almost cooked through.
6. Stir in *beurre manié.*
7. Add spinach and mint. Cook, covered, for an additional 2–3 minutes. Add salt and pepper to taste.
8. Garnish with chopped mint.

SERVES 4–6

Another Plumb-Pottage

Get two Gallons of strong Broth; put to it two Pounds of Currants, two Pounds of Raisins of the Sun, half an Ounce of Sweet Spice, a Pound of Sugar, a Quart of Claret, a Pint of Sack, the juice of three Oranges and three Lemons; thicken it with grated Biskets, or Rice Flour, with a Pound of Prunes.

The Whole Duty of a Woman

Plum Pottage. By the late seventeenth century, this fruited broth became associated with Christmas and was often called Christmas pottage. When made extremely thick by the addition of barley, bread, or sago, it was referred to as *plumb-porridge*. About the latter Saussure complains, "few foreigners find [it] to their taste . . . a great treat for English people, though I assure you not for me."

This soup is sweet and rich, so plan to serve small portions (in dainty cups, perhaps?). It is elegant both hot and cold.

6 cups strong beef broth
$\frac{3}{4}$ cup claret
$\frac{1}{3}$ cup dry sherry
juice of 1 orange (about $\frac{1}{4}$ cup)
juice of 1 small lemon (about 3 tablespoons)
$\frac{1}{2}$ cup currants
$\frac{1}{2}$ cup raisins
$\frac{1}{2}$ cup pitted prunes
2 tablespoons sugar
$\frac{1}{8}$ teaspoon mace
$\frac{1}{8}$ teaspoon freshly grated nutmeg
scant $\frac{1}{8}$ teaspoon cloves
$\frac{1}{4}$ teaspoon cinnamon
optional: 2 tablespoons (or more) rice flour or Naples biscuit crumbs (recipe, p. 142)

1. In a large soup pot, combine all ingredients except rice flour or biscuit crumbs.
2. Bring to a boil, then simmer, uncovered, for 30 minutes.
3. If you wish to thicken the soup, wet rice flour or biscuit crumbs with $\frac{1}{2}$ cup of the soup broth; then blend into soup and cook until thickened.
4. Check seasoning before serving.

SERVES 6–8

Eels Fry'd

You must scotch them very thick in, cut each Eel in eight Pieces, mix them up with Yolks of Eggs, and season them with Pepper, Salt, grated Bread, Thyme and Parsly; then flower them and fry them: You may do them a plain Way only with Flower and Salt; serve them with melted Butter and fry'd Parsly.

Charles Carter, *The Compleat City and Country Cook*

Fried Eel. This is a rather unusual recipe for eel, which was generally collared, potted, or roasted on a spit. It is quick, easy, and subtly delicious. The best way to eat the eel is to pick it up with your fingers: just chew around the central bone.

$1\frac{1}{2}$ pounds eel, skinned and cut into $1\frac{1}{2}$-inch pieces
salt and freshly ground pepper
yolk of 1 large egg
$\frac{1}{4}$ cup bread crumbs
$\frac{1}{4}$ teaspoon thyme
1 tablespoon minced fresh parsley
oil for shallow frying
garnish: lemon wedges, sprigs of parsley*

1. Rinse eel pieces and pat dry. Dust lightly with salt and pepper.
2. In a bowl, lightly beat egg yolk.
3. On a large flat plate, combine bread crumbs, thyme, and parsley.
4. Dip eel pieces in egg yolk, then roll in bread-crumb mixture.
5. In a large skillet, heat oil to sizzling.
6. Fry eel pieces about 2–3 minutes on each side, or until golden brown. Drain on paper towels.
7. Serve hot with a garnish of lemon wedges and parsley.

SERVES 4

*If you wish to garnish with fried parsley as the original recipe suggests, place small sprigs in sizzling oil to cover for 15 seconds; then drain on paper towels. As for the melted butter, it seems like gilding the lily to me.

Ramkins of Capons

Take the brawny white Part of your Fowl, and mince it, and beat it in a Mortar with as much Parmesan Cheese or good Cheshire; beat in a little grated Bread, and put in a little Cream, and the Yolks of 2 or 3 Eggs; make Toasts of Bread, French is best, and toast them, and lay this Stuff over them; work it up with a little Pepper and Nutmeg; put them in a Patty-pan, and toast them over with an hot Iron till enough.

Charles Carter, *The Complete Practical Cook*

Savory Toasts. For the Flemish, a *rammeken* was made of toasted bread and cheese, and this is why Carter probably chose the name for his cheese-chicken paste spread on toast. Years later, the bread base was eliminated and the mixture baked in the little porcelain dishes we now call ramekins.

Ramkins may easily be made a few hours in advance and then popped under the broiler just before needed. They make a fine hors d'oeuvre or side dish.

1-pound chicken breast, skinned and boned
$\frac{1}{2}$ cup freshly grated Parmesan or Cheshire cheese*
$\frac{1}{4}$ cup fresh bread crumbs
yolks of 2 large eggs
2 tablespoons heavy cream
1 large loaf French bread, very thinly sliced
freshly grated nutmeg
freshly ground pepper

1. Try to get your butcher to run the chicken breast through a grinder; otherwise, mince it very fine and pound it to a paste with a mortar and pestle or purée it in a blender.
2. In a bowl, combine chicken with cheese, bread crumbs, egg yolks, and cream.
3. Place bread slices on a baking sheet. Toast them in a 350°F oven for 5–7 minutes.
4. Spread a thin layer of chicken mixture on each bread slice. Dust lightly with nutmeg and pepper.
5. Place toasts under the broiler for 3–4 minutes, or until golden brown.

Y I E L D : approximately 2 dozen toasts

*For this recipe, Parmesan works best. If you do use Cheshire, be sure to add some salt to bring out the flavor.

To Farce Mushrooms

Make a Farce with Veal, Bacon, Beef Marrow, French Roll soaked in Cream and the Yolks of two Eggs, seasoned with Salt, Pepper, and Nutmeg. Pick the Mushrooms well, and pull off the Stalks, then farce them with this Farce; put them in a Tart-pan, and bake them in an Oven: When done, dish them, and pour to them some Beef-gravy. You may, if you think proper, make your Farce of the Flesh of Fish.

Adam's Luxury, and Eve's Cookery

Stuffed Mushrooms. These stuffed mushrooms are quite a treat. They may be prepared in advance and baked just before needed. For an interesting variation, substitute raw fish pounded to a paste for the veal and proceed as directed.

$1/4$ pound lean bacon, minced
2 tablespoons milk or cream
yolk of 1 large egg

$^{1}/_{4}$ teaspoon salt
$^{1}/_{8}$ teaspoon freshly ground pepper
$^{1}/_{8}$ teaspoon freshly grated nutmeg
$^{1}/_{4}$ cup diced French bread
$^{3}/_{4}$ pound ground veal
2 tablespoons bone marrow, crumbled*
18 large mushrooms, wiped clean
optional: $^{1}/_{2}$ cup gravy (recipe, p. 132)

1. In a skillet, fry bacon until crisp. Drain and set aside.
2. In a bowl, combine milk, egg yolk, and seasonings. Add bread. Mash until liquid is absorbed and bread is soft.
3. Add bacon, veal, and marrow. Blend as you would a meat loaf. Check seasoning.
4. Remove stems from mushrooms. Reserve them for another use.
5. Heap each mushroom cap with stuffing, smoothing off the mound of filling with the side of a knife.
6. Bake stuffed mushrooms on a greased baking sheet at 375°F about 10 minutes, or until mushrooms are soft.
7. Place mushrooms on a serving platter. Pour gravy over them, if you wish.

SERVES 6–8

*You may poke marrow out of beef bones with a fork or the tip of a knife, or ask your butcher to hack open the bones so you can get at the marrow more easily.

To Make a Patty of Mushrooms

Your Mushrooms being fresh-gather'd, well pick'd and wash'd, put them in a Sawce-pan with a Quarter of a Pound of Butter, a little minc'd Parsley, a little Pepper and Salt, a little Slice of Bacon; stick with four Cloves, a whole Onion; cover it up close, and stew them over the Fire, shake on them a Dust of Flower, giving them a Shake now and then as they stew, that they burn not; when their own Liquor comes to be as thick about 'em as a good Cream, throw out the whole Onion and Bacon, and set them to cook; then sheet a little Tart-pan, the Bigness of your Plate, with good fine Paste, such as you use for Tarts; let it be as thick as a Halfpenny, then pour on your Cold Mushrooms, and cover it with another Sheet of Paste and bake it three Quarters of an Hour before you want it. Cut off your Cover, and squeeze in half a Lemon, shake it together, and so serve it. Or you may bake it without a Cover, but then you must throw over your Mushrooms, a little brown Raspings of a French Roll; when it is bak'd, squeeze over half a Lemon. So serve it. Your Mushrooms being prepar'd as aforesaid, you may likewise put them into Pattypans, to garnish a Fricassee of Chickens; or any Ragoo of Beef, Mutton or Veal. Your Mushroom Patty aforesaid, is proper for second Course.

Patrick Lamb, *Royal Cookery*

Mushroom Tart. Patrick Lamb was Queen Anne's master cook, and his instruction to pierce an onion with cloves for use as a flavoring agent clearly reflects the French influence on aristocratic English cuisine. The "French Roll" mentioned later in the recipe would have been a small white loaf enriched with eggs and butter, not unlike the Jewish *challah.*

If you like mushrooms, you will surely consider this *patty* a classic appetizer or side dish.

pie pastry (see step 1, below)
4 tablespoons butter
1 pound mushrooms, wiped clean and sliced
thick slice bacon
1 small onion, peeled and stuck with 2 cloves
2 tablespoons finely chopped fresh parsley
$\frac{1}{2}$ teaspoon salt
$\frac{1}{8}$ teaspoon freshly ground pepper
1 tablespoon flour
$\frac{1}{4}$ cup toasted bread crumbs
$\frac{1}{2}$ small lemon

1. Line a 9-inch pie plate or flan ring, or 6 individual tart tins, with pastry. Prebake, covered with aluminum foil and filled with dried beans, at 375°F for 10 minutes. Remove beans and foil. Bake for an additional 10 minutes. Set aside.
2. In a large saucepan, melt butter. Add mushrooms, bacon, onion, parsley, salt, and pepper. Sprinkle with flour.
3. Cover and cook over low heat for 15 minutes, stirring occasionally.
4. Remove bacon and onion. Cool mixture to room temperature.
5. Spoon mixture into pastry shell(s). Sprinkle with bread crumbs.
6. Bake at 350°F for 15 minutes.
7. If using flan ring or tart tins, turn mushroom tart(s) out of molds. Squeeze on lemon juice just before serving.

SERVES 6

OF MEAT, FISH, AND SAVOURY PIES

A Cheshire Pork-Pye

Take a Loin of Pork, skin it, cut it into Stakes, season it with Salt, Nutmeg, and Pepper; make a good Crust, lay a layer of Pork, and then a large Layer of Pippins pared and cored, a little Sugar, enough to sweeten the Pye, then another layer of Pork; put in half a Pint of white Wine, lay some Butter on the Top, and close your Pye: If your Pye be large, it will take a Pint of white Wine.

Hannah Glasse, *The Art of Cookery*

Cheshire Pork Pie. Pies containing pippins and other varieties of apple were so popular in the north of England that canal boats, after delivering coal to the south, returned home full of the fruits grown in Kent and other southern orchards.

The recorded tradition of combining fruit and meat stems back to the Middle Ages, but the name *Cheshire pork-pye* indicates that this particular combination of pippins and pork was a regional specialty. Most likely a pie of this type would have been baked in a freestanding hot-water crust (recipe, p. 160), but you may prefer to use a conventional pie plate and flaky pastry.

pie pastry for shell and lid (see step 1, below)

1¾ pounds boneless loin of pork, cut into ½-inch dice

salt and freshly ground pepper

freshly grated nutmeg

4 medium cooking apples, peeled, cored, and sliced

1 tablespoon sugar

½ cup white wine

2 tablespoons butter, cut into small bits

1 egg yolk plus 1 tablespoon milk, beaten

1. Line a 10-inch pie plate or shallow 1½-quart casserole with pie pastry. Set aside. Roll out pastry for the lid and refrigerate until needed.

2. Dust diced pork lightly with salt, pepper, and nutmeg.

3. Place half the pork in pastry shell.

5. Cover pork with apple slices. Sprinkle with sugar.

6. Cover apple slices with remaining pork.

7. Pour wine over pork. Arrange bits of butter on top.

8. Cover with pastry lid and crimp edges. Decorate lid with pastry cutouts, if you wish.

9. Paint lid with egg-yolk–milk mixture. Slash lid to allow steam to escape.

10. Bake at 375°F for 1 hour and 15 minutes. If pastry becomes too brown, cover with aluminum foil or baking parchment.

11. Let pie stand at room temperature about 5 minutes before serving.

SERVES 6–8

A Harrico of Mutton

Take a Neck or Loin of Mutton, cut it into six Pieces, flour it, and fry it Brown on both Sides in the Stew-pan, then pour out all the Fat, put in some Turnips and Carrots cut like Dice, two Dozen of Chestnuts blanched, two or three Lettuces small, six little round Onions, a Bundle of Sweet Herbs, some Pepper and Salt, and two or three Blades of Mace; cover it close, and let it stew for an Hour, then take off the Fat and dish it up.

Hannah Glasse, *The Art of Cookery*

Mutton Stew. A *harrico* was a stew made of mutton, vegetables, and sweet herbs. The chestnuts included in this recipe are a particularly lovely touch. Like most stews, this *harrico* tastes even better the next day.

$4\frac{1}{2}$ pounds (ready-to-cook weight, bones intact) neck and loin of mutton or lamb
$\frac{1}{4}$ cup flour
oil for shallow frying
bouquet garni: 3–4 sprigs parsley, 1–2 sprigs thyme, bay leaf*
$\frac{1}{4}$ teaspoon ground mace
$\frac{3}{4}$ pound pearl onions, peeled and halved
1 pound small turnips, peeled and diced
3 large carrots, scrubbed and thinly sliced
2 small heads Boston (butter) lettuce, washed, trimmed, and finely shredded
2 dozen blanched chestnuts**
salt and freshly ground pepper

1. Have your butcher trim meat and cut it into 2-inch chunks, bones intact.
2. Dredge meat in flour.
3. In a large heavy pot, fry meat in hot oil until brown.
4. If you wish, drain meat on paper towels and pour off any fat left in pot. Return meat to pot.
5. Add *bouquet garni,* mace, vegetables, and chestnuts. Season with salt and pepper.
6. Cook, covered, over low heat for 2 hours and 40 minutes, or until meat and vegetables are tender. Stir every 30 minutes. (If your pot doesn't have a tight-fitting lid, cover it with a large piece of aluminum foil; then place lid on top of foil to hold it in place. It is easier to assure the slow cooking of this stew if you place the pot on a flame tamer.)
7. Skim off fat.
8. Check seasoning. Remove *bouquet garni* (if you have used one) before serving.

NOTE: If, after the first 30 minutes of cooking, your stew seems very dry, you may add $\frac{1}{4}$ to $\frac{1}{2}$ cup mutton or beef broth.

SERVES 6

*Make a *bouquet garni* by placing parsley, thyme, and bay leaf in a piece of clean cheesecloth. Tie *bouquet garni* securely with string. Alternatively, you may add 3 tablespoons finely chopped fresh parsley, 1 tablespoon finely chopped fresh thyme (or 1 teaspoon dried thyme), and 1 whole bay leaf directly to stew.

**To blanch chestnuts, slit them and drop into boiling water. Cook for 5 minutes. Run them under cold water and remove peels immediately. It is wise to boil an extra 4–5 chestnuts, as some usually turn out to be rotten. If you don't have fresh chestnuts, dried chestnuts which have been soaked in water for 1 hour and parboiled for 10 minutes may be substituted.

Collar'd Mutton, Veal, or Lamb

Take a Breast and bone it, then wash the Inside with Egg; season with Nutmeg, Pepper, Salt, and Mace, lay a Sheet of Bacon over it and some force-meat half inch thick; then roll it up tight and skewer it with six Skewers and tie it with Packthread, and either bake it, stove it, or boil or roast it: You may cut it in Slices or send it whole, garnished with Patties or Cutlets; sauce it with good gravy, Butter, and Juice of an Orange; so serve away quick and hot.

Charles Carter, *The Compleat City and Country Cook*

Stuffed Veal or Lamb Roast. Collared meats were rolled up tightly around a stuffing and bound securely with "packthread," then roasted or baked. When boiled, they were wrapped in a protective cloth called a collar.

This stuffed roast is a dramatic dish. You may wish to surround it with small mushroom tarts, as Carter's recipe suggests.

4 pounds boned breast of veal or lamb, pounded flat
1 large egg, beaten
salt and freshly ground pepper
freshly grated nutmeg
mace
$\frac{1}{4}$ pound lean bacon or smoked ham, thinly sliced

$^3/_4$ pound forcemeat (recipe, p. 82) or sweet sausage removed from casing

optional garnish: mushroom tarts (recipe, p. 72)

FOR GRAVY:

$^1/_4$ cup dry white wine

1 tablespoon butter

juice of 1 orange (generous $^1/_4$ cup)

1. Preheat oven to 450°F.
2. Paint lean side of veal with egg. Dust with seasonings.
3. If using bacon, fry until cooked but still limp. Drain.
4. If using sausage or a forcemeat containing pork, brown it. Drain.
5. Spread forcemeat on veal.
6. Place a layer of cooked bacon or smoked ham on top of forcemeat.
7. Roll up veal in the shape of a long sausage and fasten with skewers. Wind string tightly around roll, tying knots at intervals.
8. Set veal in a roasting pan and place in oven.
9. Reduce temperature immediately to 350°F and bake for 2 hours, or until internal temperature of roast registers 170°F on a meat thermometer.
10. Remove roast from oven. Remove skewers and discard string. Let stand on a serving platter for 5–10 minutes before slicing. Garnish with mushroom tarts, if you wish.
11. Meanwhile, prepare gravy: Pour pan juices into a small saucepan. Skim off fat and add wine. Boil until reduced to $^1/_2$ cup. Stir in butter and orange juice. Serve in a sauceboat.

SERVES 6–8

For the Forc'd Meat-Balls

Take Rabbet, Veal, or Pork; shred it very fine, with a few Chives, Sweet Herbs, and a little Spinage to make them look Green; season them with Salt, Pepper, Mace, Anchovies, Marrow or Beef-suet; cut all these very fine together, and bind them with a little Flour and the Yolk of an Egg, and rowl up some long, some round; fry them brown and crisp, or stew them as you please.

Henry Howard, *England's Newest Way in All Sorts of Cookery*

Forcemeat Balls. *Forc'd meat* was usually ground and used as a stuffing or for sausages, but it was sometimes formed into balls or cylinders and fried, or stewed in pottages (recipe, p. 62). Probably the most unusual use of forcemeat can be seen in Hannah Glasse's instructions "to dress larks pear fashion": "Wrap up every lark in forcemeat, and shape them like a pear, stick one leg in the top like the stalk. . . ."

I assure you, the recipe below uses *forc'd meat* in a much more conventional way.

1 pound ground rabbit, veal, or pork

2 teaspoons chopped chives*

1 teaspoon dried marjoram or summer savory

½ cup spinach, washed, trimmed, and finely chopped

½ teaspoon salt

⅛ teaspoon freshly ground pepper

generous pinch mace

6 anchovy fillets, finely chopped

optional: 1 tablespoon beef marrow or suet, finely chopped

2 teaspoons flour

yolk of 1 large egg

oil or lard for shallow frying or *pease pottage* (recipe, p. 62)

1. In a bowl, combine all ingredients except oil.
2. Shape into 10–12 balls or cylinders.
3. Fry in oil or lard until brown or cook in *pease pottage*. Drain before serving.

YIELD: about 1 dozen forcemeat balls

*Freeze-dried chives may be used if fresh are unavailable, but first soak them in ¼ cup warm water. You may substitute the green ends of scallions, finely chopped.

Scotch Colaps —Very Good Ones

Take a Leg of Veal slice it very thin & beat ym well wt ye back of a shreding knife Fry ym prety brown wt as little butter as you can yn take half a pint of strong broth wt a quarter of a pint of beef gravey & as much clarid wine put alltogether with 10 or 12 mincth Anchovey, half a Lemon sliced & a lettel pece of ye peel, a Nutmeg, a lettel Mace & solt, an Onion & give ym a boile or too in a frying pan yn put in to ym ye yolks of 2 eggs well beat & a Lettel fresh butter shaking ym constantly till ye sauce be of a prety thickness. So send it up.

> Elizabeth Wainwright, *The Receipt Book of a Lady of the Reign of Queen Anne*

Veal Scaloppini with Anchovy-Wine Sauce. Although collops in the Middle Ages were thick slices of bacon (often served with eggs), by the late seventeenth century scotch collops were any type of sliced meat pounded thin, like their Italian relatives, *scaloppini.*

The sauce may be prepared in advance up to the last step of whisking in the egg yolks, which should be done just before serving.

1 cup strong beef broth
$\frac{1}{2}$ cup gravy (recipe, p. 132)*

*You may substitute an additional $\frac{1}{2}$ cup broth for gravy.

½ cup claret
2 tablespoons finely chopped onion
4 (or more) anchovy fillets, chopped
½ large lemon, thinly sliced
⅛ teaspoon freshly grated nutmeg
pinch mace
equal parts clarified butter and oil for shallow frying
veal scallops for six, pounded thin
salt and freshly ground pepper
yolks of 2 large eggs, beaten
1 tablespoon butter

1. In a saucepan, combine broth, gravy, claret, onion, anchovies, lemon slices, nutmeg, and mace. Simmer for 20 minutes, then set aside to cool slightly.
2. Meanwhile, in a large skillet, heat clarified butter and oil.
3. Dust veal scallops lightly with salt and pepper. Fry them quickly (less than 1 minute on each side) in the very hot fat (clarified butter and oil). Fry only 2–3 scallops at one time; remove them to a serving platter and keep warm.
4. Whisk egg yolks into sauce.
5. Pour sauce into skillet in which veal scallops were fried. Cook over medium heat, adding butter and whisking, until sauce thickens. Take care not to boil or sauce will curdle.
6. Adjust seasoning. Pour sauce over meat, or serve it on the side in a sauceboat.

SERVES 6

To Friggassee Chickens

Take four Chickens or Rabbits: take ye skin of & cut them in small pieces, crack the bones very well, season them with salt & frey ym prety brown in Fresh Butter. Then take them out of the pan & ly them whear the butter may drayn from them: then take a pint of white wine or a pinte of alle & half as much watter. Let them stue till thay be allmost stud away, then take three egges yolks & beat them very well; then put a pint of Cream to them, a grated Nutmeg & and littel shred onyon, salt, & a littel shred time a Lump of butter as beg as a wall nut. Put it in the stew to your meat & when enough shake them very well together & go send them up.

Elizabeth Wainwright, *The Receipt Book of a Lady of the Reign of Queen Anne*

Chicken Fricassee. A *friggassee* (from the French *fricasser,* to mince and cook in sauce) was a rich stew whose main ingredient might be tripe, veal, "ox palates," pigeon, sweetbreads, artichoke bottoms, or, in this case, chicken or rabbit. The sauce base was usually wine or broth; it was thickened with cream, butter, and egg yolks, flavored with nutmeg or sweet herbs, and sometimes given a sharp edge with pickles, anchovies, and capers.

To take best advantage of the delicious sauce, serve this dish over rice.

5-pound chicken or rabbit, cut into small pieces, skin removed
salt
4 tablespoons butter
1 cup dry white wine
$\frac{1}{8}$ teaspoon freshly grated nutmeg
$\frac{1}{4}$ teaspoon thyme
1 tablespoon finely minced onion
1–2 tablespoons additional butter
yolk of 1 large egg
1 cup heavy cream

1. Wash chicken pieces and pat dry. Dust with salt.
2. In a large heavy pot, melt 4 tablespoons butter. Brown chicken. Set on paper towels to drain.
3. In the same pot, combine wine, nutmeg, thyme, onion, and additional butter. Bring to a boil.
4. Add chicken. Return to a boil, then cover and simmer, stirring occasionally, for 40 minutes, or until chicken is done.
5. Remove chicken to a platter and reserve in a warm place.
6. Beat together egg yolk and cream. Whisk into sauce and cook over very low heat about 30 seconds, or until sauce thickens. Take care not to boil or sauce will curdle.
7. Check seasoning. Pour sauce over chicken.

SERVES 6–8

Chickens Forced with Oysters

Lard and truss them: make a forcing with Oysters, Sweet-breads, Parsley, Truffles, Mushrooms and Onions; chop these together, and season it; mix it with a Piece of Butter and the Yolk of an Egg; then tie them at both Ends and roast them; then make for them a Ragoo, and garnish them with sliced Lemon.

The Complete Family Piece

Chicken with Oyster Stuffing. In the eighteenth century, oyster stuffing became very fashionable; oysters were plentiful, and there was no longer a pervasive religious concern for dividing the calendar into fish and flesh days.

Since truffles are so expensive, I have left them out, but if you happen to have one around the house . . .

$\frac{1}{2}$ pound sweetbreads, diced*
5-pound roasting chicken
salt and freshly ground pepper
12 shucked oysters in their juice
6 large mushrooms, quartered
2 tablespoons finely minced onion
2 tablespoons chopped parsley
2 tablespoons butter, cut into small bits

yolk of 1 large egg
garnish: 1 lemon, thinly sliced
optional: *ragoo* (recipe, p. 134)

1. In a saucepan, soak sweetbreads in ice water for 20 minutes. Add $\frac{1}{2}$ teaspoon salt and bring to a gentle boil. Reduce heat and simmer for 10 minutes, then refresh in cold water. Remove any tubes or outer membranes. Pat dry and dice.
2. Wash chicken and pat dry. Season with salt and pepper inside and out.
3. In a bowl, combine sweetbreads with remaining ingredients.
4. Close neck cavity of chicken by sewing or with skewers.
5. Stuff chicken, tilting to pour in liquid.
6. Close bottom end of cavity by sewing or with skewers.
7. Roast at 375°F about 2 hours. Chicken is done if juices run clear when plumpest part is pricked.
8. Garnish with lemon slices. Serve with or without *ragoo*.

   NOTE: If you skim the fat off the pan juices and combine them with the juices given off as the chicken is carved, you'll have a most delicious gravy.

SERVES 5–6

* Sweetbreads must generally be ordered from the butcher in advance, and it might be difficult to buy them in small quantity. If you wish to leave them out, use a few extra mushrooms or $\frac{1}{4}$ cup bread crumbs. You will still find the stuffing unusual and delicious.

To Broil Trouts

Wash and gut them very clean, dry them with a Napkin, sprinkle them over with melted Butter and Salt, then broil them over a gentle Fire, and Turn them very often. Serve them with a Sauce made of Butter, a little Flour, Salt, Pepper, Nutmeg, some Capers, an Anchovy, and a very little Water and Vinegar. Turn the Sauce on the Stove 'till it is of a right Thickness, then lay your Trouts in a Dish, pour the Sauce upon them, and serve them.

John Middleton, *Five Hundred New Receipts*

Trout with Anchovy Sauce. The acceptance of the fork in England, in the late seventeenth century, spelled doom to medieval "spooned" fish stews; it then became practical to serve whole broiled fish with interesting sauces like the one below.

$^1\!/_4$ pound butter
2 teaspoons flour
4 anchovy fillets, chopped
2 teaspoons capers
1 teaspoon water
1 teaspoon (or more) wine vinegar
salt and freshly ground pepper
freshly grated nutmeg
4 whole small brook trout, cleaned
garnish: lemon wedges

1. In a heavy saucepan, melt butter.
2. Whisk in flour.
3. Add remaining ingredients except trout. Simmer for 10 minutes.
4. Broil trout and pour on sauce. Garnish with lemon wedges and serve immediately.

CREATIVE ANACHRONISM: If you'd like to use fillets instead of whole fish, here is an interesting variation of this recipe: Prepare sauce. Place fillets next to each other on a large heatproof serving dish and pour sauce over them. Cover fillets with a large piece of aluminum foil, tucking edges tightly under dish. Rest dish on top of a large pot three quarters full of boiling water, and steam fish for 18 minutes. I enjoy using this method, as the fish absorbs the flavor of the sauce and the serving platter is hot when it is brought to the table.

SERVES 4

A Flounder Pie, Savoury

Take large Flounders, and draw them, and cut off their Heads, Fin[s], and Tails, and hack them on the Bellies, and wash them over with the Yolk of an Egg; season them with Thyme, Parsley, Pepper, Salt, Nutmeg, and Ginger; lay them in your Coffin, and lay some Forc'd-meat of Fish, and some Oysters over them; lay another Row of Flounders, put Butter over them, and bake them open: when bak'd, take out the Fat, and make a Leer with Wine, Anchovies, a little Shallot, and some Oysters cut in Pieces, and some Capers minc'd. . . .

Charles Carter, *The Complete Practical Cook*

Savory Flounder Pie. Since whole flounders are called for in the original recipe, a large freestanding pie made with hot-water pastry is probably what Carter had in mind. It is difficult to be certain, though, as pie tins lined with rich flaky pastry were becoming more and more common during this period. Unless I am in the mood to make this pie in a fanciful shape, I generally prefer to bake it in a round pie plate.

8-inch unbaked pie pastry shell
2 pounds fillets of flounder
yolk of 1 large egg, beaten
salt and freshly ground pepper
freshly grated nutmeg
$\frac{1}{2}$-pound fish fillet of your choice, beaten to a paste

8 oysters, chopped

2 tablespoons minced parsley

1 teaspoon dried thyme

1 teaspoon finely grated ginger

scant $\frac{1}{4}$ teaspoon salt

$\frac{1}{8}$ teaspoon freshly ground pepper

2 tablespoons butter, cut into bits

$\frac{1}{2}$ cup dry white wine

2 anchovy fillets, chopped

4 oysters, chopped

1 tablespoon minced shallots

1 teaspoon capers

1. Prebake pastry shell, covered with aluminum foil and filled with beans, at 375°F for 15 minutes. Remove beans and foil. Bake for an additional 10 minutes. Set aside.
2. Paint flounder fillets with egg yolk. Dust lightly with salt, pepper, and nutmeg.
3. In a bowl, combine fish paste, oysters, parsley, thyme, ginger, scant $\frac{1}{4}$ teaspoon salt, and $\frac{1}{8}$ teaspoon pepper.
4. Place half the flounder fillets in pastry shell. Spread seasoned fish paste on top, then cover with remaining fillets. Dot with butter bits. Bake at 350°F about 15 minutes, or until fish flakes.
5. Meanwhile, in a saucepan, combine remaining ingredients for sauce. Simmer for 15 minutes.
6. Pour sauce over pie, or serve on the side in a sauceboat.

SERVES 4–6

Mince Pies

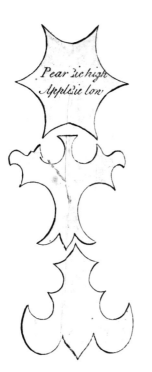

Pear *kehigh*
Apple ie low

Shred 2 lb of meate with 3 lb of beefe suett very small season it with a qt of an Ounce of Cloves & mace halfe as much Cinnamon one nutmegg, halfe a lb of Canded Orange Lemon, & Citron sliced 2 pippins shred, halfe a lb of sugar a glasse of sacke ye Juice of 2 Lemons or veriuice 2 or 3 penyworth of fruit if you love it full mix all together, & bis kitt to fill yr pies.

Alice Fleming, *Manuscript Cookery Book*

Mincemeat Pie. There is a beautiful copper plate in Henry Howard's *England's Newest Way in All Sorts of Cookery,* which depicts nine raised molds for "The Several Fashions of Mince Pyes": a heart, a spade, a kidney, an oval, and others more fanciful. If you own a fluted-edged raised pie mold, this is a good time to use it, or if you prefer, bake the filling in a pastry-lined loaf pan. This pie tastes better hot, but it may be served cold as well.

$\frac{1}{2}$ cup dry sherry
$\frac{1}{2}$ teaspoon cloves
$\frac{1}{4}$ teaspoon mace
$\frac{1}{2}$ teaspoon cinnamon
$\frac{1}{4}$ teaspoon nutmeg
$1\frac{1}{2}$ pounds lean chuck, cut into $\frac{1}{4}$-inch dice

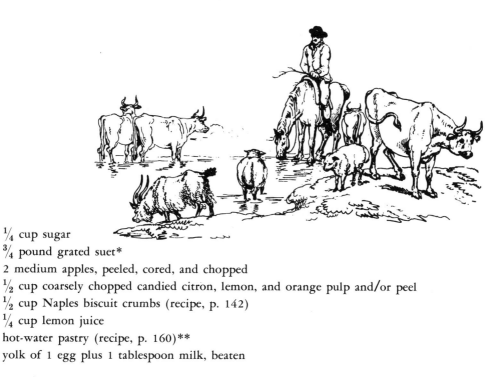

¼ cup sugar
¾ pound grated suet*
2 medium apples, peeled, cored, and chopped
½ cup coarsely chopped candied citron, lemon, and orange pulp and/or peel
½ cup Naples biscuit crumbs (recipe, p. 142)
¼ cup lemon juice
hot-water pastry (recipe, p. 160)**
yolk of 1 egg plus 1 tablespoon milk, beaten

*I have considerably reduced the proportion of suet to meat. If you wish to adhere more closely to the original recipe, use 2 pounds suet.
**If you prefer, you may make this pie with the pastry crust of your choice.

1. In a large bowl, combine sherry, spices, and sugar. Add meat and stir to coat.

2. Marinate meat in refrigerator for 12 hours, turning occasionally.

3. Add remaining ingredients except pastry and egg-yolk–milk mixture. Blend thoroughly. Set aside.

4. Prepare hot-water pastry as directed on page 160. Press pastry either into a raised pie mold with removable bottom and sides and approximately a $1\frac{1}{2}$-quart capacity, a very well greased 9- by 5- by 3-inch loaf pan, or a $1\frac{1}{2}$-quart casserole.

5. Fill pastry shell with meat mixture.

6. Cover with pastry lid and crimp edges. Slash decoratively to allow steam to escape. Arrange pastry cutouts in an attractive design.

7. Paint lid with egg-yolk–milk mixture.

8. Place pie in a large shallow baking dish to catch drippings. (The suet tends to boil over when it is hot.)

9. Bake at 375°F for 1 hour. Reduce temperature to 325°F and bake for an additional hour. If pastry becomes too brown, cover loosely with aluminum foil.

10. When done, remove pie from oven. Let cool for 10 minutes.

11. If using a raised pie mold, remove bottom and sides. To unmold pie baked in a loaf pan, first rest the pan for a few moments in hot water while running a sharp knife between pie and sides of pan. Remove pan from water. Place a large plate on top of pie and flip over pan and plate. Gently tap bottom of pan until pie is released. Lift pan up, and gently turn pie upright.

SERVES 6–8

OF PUDDINGS

A Yorkshire Pudding

Take a Quart of Milk, four Eggs, and a little Salt, make it up into a thick Batter with Flour, like a Pancake Batter. You must have a good Piece of Meat at the Fire, take a Stew-pan and put some Dripping in, set it on the Fire; when it boils, pour in your Pudding; let it bake on the Fire till you think it is high enough, then turn a Plate upside-down in the Dripping-pan, that the Dripping may not be blacked; set your Stew-pan on it under your Meat, and let the Dripping drop on the Pudding, and the Heat of the Fire come to it, to make it of a fine Brown. When your Meat is done and sent to Table, drain all the Fat from your Pudding, and set it on the Fire again to dry a little; then slide it as dry as you can into a Dish, melt some Butter, and pour into a Cup, and set in the Middle of the Pudding. It is an exceeding good Pudding; the Gravy of the Meat eats well with it.

Hannah Glasse, *The Art of Cookery*

Yorkshire Pudding. Some say that only a Yorkshirewoman can produce a real Yorkshire pudding, but it seemed only right to make an earnest effort to reproduce this renowned English dish. The first version uses proportions suggested by the original recipe, which results in a hearty, somewhat stodgy pudding; the second, which bears no resemblance to Mrs. Glasse's instructions, produces a light, fluffy pudding perhaps more compatible with contemporary tastes. Either batter may be poured directly

into the roasting pan (if your roast is set on a rack) instead of being baked in a separate pan, but check after 12 minutes, as the pudding will probably be done more quickly if cooked this way. Serve Yorkshire pudding immediately, while it is still puffed up, and "send it forth" with butter or gravy for sauce.

1 large egg, beaten
1 cup milk
1 cup flour
$\frac{1}{2}$ teaspoon salt
$\frac{1}{4}$ teaspoon freshly grated nutmeg
$\frac{1}{4}$ teaspoon ground ginger
2–3 tablespoons pan drippings or butter

1. In a bowl, beat egg and milk until frothy.
2. Add flour gradually and continue beating.
3. Beat in salt, nutmeg, and ginger.
4. Refrigerate batter for at least 1 hour.
5. Remove batter from refrigerator. Beat for 1 minute.
6. In a 9-inch cast-iron skillet, heat pan drippings until sizzling.
7. Pour batter into the center of the skillet.
8. Bake at 375°F about 20 minutes, or until top is golden.

SERVES 6–8

2 large eggs

$\frac{3}{4}$ cup milk

$\frac{1}{4}$ cup water

$\frac{1}{2}$ cup plus 2 tablespoons flour

$\frac{1}{2}$ teaspoon salt

$\frac{1}{4}$ teaspoon freshly grated nutmeg

$\frac{1}{4}$ teaspoon ground ginger

2–3 tablespoons pan drippings or butter

1. Separate eggs. Refrigerate whites.
2. In a bowl, beat yolks for 1 minute.
3. Add milk and then water in a stream, beating all the while.
4. Add flour gradually. Continue beating.
5. Beat in salt, nutmeg, and ginger.
6. Refrigerate batter for at least 1 hour.
7. In a bowl, beat egg whites until they form stiff peaks.
8. Remove batter from refrigerator. Beat for 1 minute.
9. Fold stiff whites into batter.
10. In a 9-inch cast-iron skillet, heat pan drippings until sizzling.
11. Pour batter into the center of the skillet.
12. Bake at 375°F about 20 minutes, or until top is golden.

SERVES 6–8

Take some clean Potatoes, boil them tender, and when they are so, and clean from their Skins, break them in a Marble Mortar, till they become a Pulp; then put to them, or you might beat with them some slices of candy'd Lemons and Oranges, and beat these together with some Spices, and Lemon-Peel candy'd. Put to these some Marrow and as much Sugar, with Orange Flower Water, as you think fit. Mix all together, and then take some whole candy'd Orange-Peels, and stuff them full of the Meat, and set them upon a Dish, in a gentle Oven; and when they have stood half an hour, serve them hot, with a Sauce of Sack and Butter, and fine Sugar grated over them.

R. Bradley, *The Country Housewife and Lady's Director*

Potato Pudding. Potatoes were generally roasted with meats, and recipes like the one above are somewhat unusual in the early eighteenth century. It is difficult to know what type of potato is intended here—perhaps whatever was at hand. Batty Langley, in his *New Principles of Gardening* (1728), describes four types of potato: white kidney, white round, Lancashire (very pale reddish), and red, "the very best of all."

The following recipe was made with white baking potatoes. Certainly sweet potatoes would work just as well, but you'd probably want to reduce the amount of sugar. This pudding goes very well with roast pork or lamb.

Potatoe-Puddings, Made with Sweet-Meats from Mr. Moring, Temple Bar

3 pounds potatoes, boiled or baked, skins removed

2–3 tablespoons bone marrow, crumbled*

2–3 tablespoons sugar

$\frac{1}{2}$ cup candied lemon and orange slices, chopped

$\frac{1}{4}$ cup candied lemon or orange peel, chopped

$\frac{1}{4}$ teaspoon freshly grated nutmeg

$\frac{1}{2}$ teaspoon cinnamon

1 tablespoon orange-flower water

optional: candied orange bowls (recipe follows)

additional 1 tablespoon sugar

FOR SAUCE:

$\frac{1}{3}$ cup sherry

3 tablespoons butter

1. Mash potatoes. Stir in marrow, 2–3 tablespoons sugar, candied fruit and peel, and spices.
2. Place in a $1\frac{1}{2}$-quart casserole. Bake at 375°F for 25 minutes.
3. Remove from oven. Stir in orange-flower water.
4. If you are using candied orange bowls, fill them with pudding and place on a greased baking sheet. Otherwise, leave pudding in casserole.
5. Sprinkle casserole or orange bowls with additional sugar. Bake for an additional 5 minutes or until hot. (If using orange bowls, reduce temperature to 150°F. Be careful that they don't burn.)

   *You may poke marrow out of beef bones with a fork or the tip of a knife, or ask your butcher to hack open the bones so you can get at the marrow more easily.

6. In a small saucepan, heat sherry and butter until butter melts. Pour sauce over casserole or orange bowls, or serve in a sauceboat.

SERVES 6–8

CANDIED ORANGE BOWLS
4 large juice oranges, well scrubbed
2$\frac{1}{2}$ cups sugar
1 cup water
additional sugar

1. Cut oranges in half through the middle. Squeeze out juice and reserve for another use.
2. Gently peel away pulp to create a hollow bowl of each orange half.
3. Place bowls in a large, heavy enameled or stainless-steel pot. Add cold water to cover. Bring to a boil, then cover pot and cook over medium heat for 1 hour. Drain peel and discard water.
4. In a small saucepan, dissolve sugar in 1 cup water and boil syrup gently for 5 minutes. Scrape off sugar crystals that form on the sides of the pot and stir them into syrup.
5. Return orange bowls to large pot. Pour syrup into and around them. Cover and simmer very slowly over low heat for 2 hours.
6. Uncover pot and cook over medium heat about 50 minutes, or until syrup is almost evaporated.
7. Remove from pot. Roll in sugar to coat. Cool on a rack.

NOTE: This method may also be used to prepare candied grapefruit bowls, citrus fruit slices, or peel.

YIELD: 8 candied orange bowls

An Artichoke Pudin[g]

Take 8 artichoks boyle ym tell ye be tender yn take of all ye leves of & core & strings out yn beat ym well in a bole & forse ym through a hare sive yn have redy 6 eggs lave out 3 whits beat ym yn beat ym with ye artichoks very well yn mix ym with a pint of crame a litle salt rose water & sugar too yr tast buter yr pan well halfe an oure will bake it sarve it with sack or white wine buter & suger.

Penelope Pemberton, *Manuscript Cookery Book*

Artichoke Pudding. The globe artichoke was introduced to England during the Elizabethan period and quickly became a popular food. There is no mention of eating the leaves, but the bottoms were *friggasseed* in wine and cream or baked with fruits, marrow, and egg yolks in a pie. This unusual, perfumed pudding will long be remembered by those who appreciate the subtle flavor of the artichoke.

104

2 packages frozen artichoke hearts or 8 very large artichokes,
  leaves and chokes removed*
3 large eggs plus 3 yolks, well beaten
2 cups heavy cream
$1\frac{1}{2}$ teaspoons salt
2 teaspoons rose water
1 teaspoon (or more) sugar

FOR SAUCE:
$\frac{1}{2}$ cup sherry
2 tablespoons butter, cut into bits
sugar

1. Boil artichoke hearts in salted water to cover until they are soft.
2. In a blender, purée artichoke hearts. Pass purée through a fine-meshed strainer into a bowl. Set aside.
3. In a large bowl, combine eggs, cream, salt, rose water, and sugar. Beat until foamy.
4. Fold egg mixture into artichoke purée and pour into a buttered $1\frac{1}{2}$-quart soufflé dish or casserole.
5. Bake at 375°F for 30 minutes, or until pudding is set.
6. In a saucepan, heat sherry. Whisk in butter and sugar to taste.
7. Pour sauce over pudding, or serve on the side in a sauceboat.

SERVES 6–8

  *If you prefer, you may boil the artichokes whole, eat the flesh from the leaves, and use the cooked hearts for the pudding.

To Make a Carrot Pudding

Take a halfe a pint of cream & put to it 3 eggs weall beaten with a little rose Water a grated nutmegg & as much raw Carrots grated as you have bread mix all these weall to gether & mealt a quarter of a pound of butter & stir it well with ye rest of ye things & soe bake it in a dish you may put some orange or lemon pill in it.

Alice Fleming, *Manuscript Cookery Book*

Carrot Pudding. The carrot, a relative newcomer to the British Isles, was introduced by the Flemish during the reign of Elizabeth. These immigrants found the soil around Sandwich particularly favorable for its cultivation. That root vegetables grew to be extremely large is made clear by Mrs. Glasse, who warns her readers that old Sandwich carrots, sliced, will take two hours to boil. Perhaps that's why Alice Fleming decided to grate them raw for this pudding.

1 cup heavy cream
3 large eggs, well beaten
2 tablespoons rose water
$\frac{1}{4}$ teaspoon freshly grated nutmeg
2 cups (about $\frac{3}{4}$ pound) finely grated carrots
1 cup fresh bread crumbs
$\frac{1}{4}$ pound butter, melted
optional: grated rind of 1 large lemon or 1 small orange

1. Combine all ingredients.
2. Bake in a $1\frac{1}{2}$-quart casserole at 375°F for 30 minutes.

NOTE: My adaptation uses half the amount of bread crumbs required by the original to create a light, custard-like pudding. To follow the eighteenth-century recipe strictly, use 2 cups bread crumbs and add rose water and nutmeg to taste. The result might be described as carrot-bread pudding.

SERVES 6–8

A Boiled Plumb-Pudding

Take a Pound of Suet cut in little Pieces, not too fine, a Pound of Currants, and a Pound of Raisins stoned, eight Eggs, one half the Whites, the Crumb of a Penny-loaf grated fine, one half a Nutmeg grated, and a Tea Spoonful of beaten Ginger, a little Salt, a Pound of Flour, a Pint of Milk; beat the Eggs first, then one half the Milk, beat them together, and by degrees stir in the Flour and Bread together, then the suet, spice and Fruit, and as much Milk as will mix it all well together and very thick; boil it five Hours.

Hannah Glasse, *The Art of Cookery*

Plum Pudding. The dried plums imported by the Elizabethans were held in such esteem that the word plum was used to describe this pudding long after the prunes were replaced by raisins and currants. In fact, plum became a generic term for these other dried fruits. "'Tis not only plumbs that make a pudding," Fielding reminds us in *Don Quixote*.

For advice about a suitable pudding cloth, see p. 53.

2 large eggs plus 2 yolks, beaten
$\frac{1}{2}$ cup milk
$1\frac{1}{2}$ cups flour
$\frac{3}{4}$ cup bread crumbs
$\frac{1}{2}$ pound suet, finely chopped
1 teaspoon powdered ginger

½ teaspoon freshly grated nutmeg

⅛ teaspoon salt

1¾ cups (½ pound) currants

1½ cups (½ pound) raisins

additional ½ cup (or more) milk

additional flour

optional: sweet sauce (recipe, p. 116)

1. In a 4-quart pot, bring 3 quarts water to a rolling boil.
2. In a bowl, combine eggs and ½ cup milk.
3. Sift in flour, stirring mixture into a smooth batter.
4. Stir in bread crumbs, suet, spices, salt, currants, and raisins.
5. Add additional ½ cup milk. Batter should be very thick.
6. Wet a pudding cloth thoroughly and dust liberally with flour. Place it in another bowl, floured side up, so that the edges hang over the rim.
7. Pour batter into pudding cloth. Gather edges and secure them by tying a string around the cloth just above the point where the pudding stops bulging.
8. Lift pudding from bowl and lower it into the boiling water.
9. Boil over medium heat for 4 hours, lifting occasionally to prevent sticking. Add water as needed to keep pudding totally submerged.
10. When cooking time is up, place pudding in a colander to drain and cool slightly. Gently peel away cloth-and-flour coating.
11. Place pudding on a serving platter. Slice into wedges and serve warm, plain or accompanied with sauce.

SERVES 8–10

To Make Colliflower Pudding

Boil the Flowers in Milk, take the Tops and lay them in a Dish, then take three Jills of Cream, the Yolks of eight Eggs, and the whites of two, season it with Nutmeg, Cinnamon, Mace, Sugar, Sack or Orange-flower-Water, beat all well together, then pour it over the Colliflower, put it into the Oven, bake it as you would a Custard, and grate Sugar over it when it comes from the Oven.

Elizabeth Moxon, *English Housewifery*

Cauliflower Pudding. This combination of flavors is quite unusual; your taste buds are likely to discover aspects of themselves they never noticed before.

110

1 medium head cauliflower

1 cup milk

1 cup water

1 cup heavy cream

2 large eggs plus 1 yolk, beaten

2 teaspoons dry sherry or $\frac{1}{2}$ teaspoon orange-flower water

1 teaspoon sugar

generous $\frac{1}{4}$ teaspoon cinnamon

$\frac{1}{8}$ teaspoon freshly grated nutmeg

pinch mace

1 additional tablespoon sugar

1. Wash cauliflower. Pat dry and cut into flowerets, discarding stalk.
2. In a saucepan, combine milk and water. Bring to a boil. Cook cauliflower, covered, over medium heat for 12 minutes.
3. Drain, then set cauliflower in a small casserole with flowerets all turning up, recreating the shape of the cauliflower head.
4. In a bowl, combine remaining ingredients except additional sugar. Pour over cauliflower.
5. Bake, uncovered, at 325°F for 30 minutes, or until pudding is set.
6. Sprinkle with additional sugar just before serving.

SERVES 4–6

To Make an Apple Pudding

Take twelve large Pipins, pare them, and take out the Cores, put them into a Sauce-pan, with four or five Spoonfuls of Water, boil them till they are soft and thick; then beat them well, stir in a quarter of a Pound of Butter, a Pound of Loaf-sugar, the juice of 3 lemons, the Peel of two Lemons cut thin, and beat fine in a Mortar, the Yolks of 8 Eggs beat; mix well together, bake it in a slack Oven, when it is near done, throw over a little fine Sugar. You may bake it in Puff-paste, as you do the other Puddings.

Hannah Glasse, *The Art of Cookery*

Apple Pudding. The tart lemon flavor is an exciting addition to this smooth, sweet apple pudding. Served with roasted meat, it becomes a fine variation of applesauce. Offered hot or cold with heavy cream, apple pudding makes a memorable dessert. You might wish to bake it in a puff-pastry shell, as the recipe suggests, or you can pipe it into prebaked vol-au-vent pastries— but the latter would be a creative anachronism as far as I know.

6 large cooking apples, peeled, cored, and sliced
$\frac{1}{3}$ cup water
4 tablespoons butter, cut into bits
$\frac{1}{2}$ cup (or more) sugar
rind of 1 large lemon, finely grated
juice of $1\frac{1}{2}$ large lemons
yolks of 4 large eggs, well beaten
2 tablespoons additional sugar

1. Place apples and water in a pot. Cover and poach over medium heat, tossing occasionally, until apples are soft.
2. Purée apples in a food mill or blender.
3. Stir in butter, $\frac{1}{2}$ cup sugar, lemon rind, and lemon juice. Add more sugar if mixture is too tart. Cool to room temperature.
4. Fold in egg yolks.
5. Pour into buttered casserole and bake at 350°F for 1 hour.
6. Sprinkle with additional sugar and return to oven for 15 minutes.

SERVES 8

To Make a Frute Pudin[g]

Take a pound of rasins & a pound of corans, 6 eggs well beat with a Glas of Sack & a nutmeg. Mix all theas together & tey in a Cloth. So let it boile 6 hours & serve it up with sweet sauce.

Elizabeth Wainwright, *The Receipt Book of a Lady of the Reign of Queen Anne*

Fruit Pudding. Here is a pudding held together by an egg-and-sherry custard rather than the more traditional suet and bread. It is much lighter as a result, but plan to serve thin slices, as it would still be considered rich by today's standards. A small piece of pudding and roasted meat would make good companions, but many would prefer this pudding for dessert.

For advice about a suitable pudding cloth, see p. 53.

114

3 large eggs
$\frac{1}{2}$ cup dry sherry
$\frac{1}{2}$ teaspoon freshly grated nutmeg
$1\frac{1}{2}$ cups raisins
$1\frac{1}{2}$ cups currants
$\frac{1}{4}$ cup flour
sweet sauce (recipe follows)

1. In a 4-quart pot, bring 3 quarts water to a rolling boil.
2. In a large bowl, whisk eggs, sherry, and nutmeg until foamy.
3. Add raisins and currants. Stir to coat.
4. Wet a pudding cloth thoroughly and dust liberally with flour. Place it in another bowl, floured side up, so that the edges hang over the rim.
5. Spoon the mixture into pudding cloth. Gather edges and secure them by tying a string around the cloth just above the point where the pudding stops bulging.
6. Lift pudding from bowl and lower it into the boiling water.
7. Boil over medium heat for 2 hours, lifting occasionally to prevent sticking. Add water as needed to keep pudding totally submerged.
8. When cooking time is up, place pudding in a colander to drain and cool slightly. Gently peel away cloth-and-flour coating.
9. Place pudding on a small serving platter. Slice into wedges and serve warm, accompanied with sauce.

SERVES 6–8

115

SWEET SAUCE
$\frac{1}{2}$ cup dry sherry
4 tablespoons butter, cut into bits
sugar

1. In a saucepan, heat sherry.
2. Whisk in butter and sugar to taste.
3. Serve in a small pitcher or sauceboat.

CREATIVE ANACHRONISM: Store leftover sweet sauce in refrigerator. Reheat and use instead of maple syrup over pancakes.

YIELD: 1 cup

OF SALLADS, PICKLING, AND KITCHEN-GARDEN STUFF

To Dress a Sallad

After you have duly proportion'd the Herbs, take two thirds of Oil of Olives, one third of Vinegar, some hard Eggs cut small, both the Whites and Yolks, a little Salt, and some Mustard, all which must be well mixed, and poured over the sallad, having first cut the large Herbs, such as Celery, Endive, Cabbage-Lettuce, but none of the small ones: Then mix all well together, that it may be ready just when you want to use it, for the oil will make it presently soften, and lost its Briskness.

Adam's Luxury, and Eve's Cookery

Georgian Salad. The priority accorded *sallad* in the late seventeenth century is questioned in Evelyn's rhyme:
> *The Sallet, which of old came in at last,*
> *Why now with it begin we our Repast?*

Such fine salads as the one below explain why no one wanted to wait.

SALAD GREENS:

Boston (butter) lettuce, shredded
celery stalks and leaves, chopped
endive, shredded
fresh herbs (parsley, dill, mint, thyme), chopped

FOR DRESSING:

$\frac{2}{3}$ cup olive oil
$\frac{1}{3}$ cup wine vinegar
$\frac{1}{4}$ teaspoon salt
1 teaspoon mustard (recipe, p. 124)
1 hard-boiled egg, finely chopped

1. Wash salad greens and dry thoroughly.
2. In a bowl or bottle, combine ingredients for dressing. Blend well.
3. Just before serving, pour dressing as needed over greens. Toss to coat.

NOTE: Dressing may be refrigerated for a few weeks in a bottle with a tight-fitting lid.

YIELD: 1 cup

Salmogundy

Mince very fine two boiled or roasted Chickens or Veal, which you like best: Mince also very small the Yolks and the whites of hard Eggs by themselves: shred also the Pulp of Lemon very small; then lay in the Dish a Layer of minced Meat, a Layer of the Yolks, and then a Layer of the whites of Eggs, over which a Layer of Anchovies, and on them a Layer of the Shred Pulp of Lemon, next a Layer of Pickles, then a Layer of Sorrel, and last of all a Layer of Spinach and Cloves of Garlic or of Shalots shred small.

The Country Magazine

Salmogundy. *Salmogundy* is an odd and fetching word whose origin is obscure. The variants are amusing: *salamongundy, salladmagundy, Solomon Gundy, salmagundy.* As they all begin with *sal*, we can assume that the beginning of the word refers to the salted fish which is an essential part of every recipe.

These instructions are somewhat unusual in placing the greens on top, and you may prefer to combine ingredients as you would for a chef's salad. Mrs. Glasse's advice on *salmogundy* may come in handy: "If you have not all these ingredients, set out your plates or saucers with just what you fancy." Pickled herring was often used instead of anchovies.

120

2$\frac{1}{2}$ cups diced, cooked chicken or veal, seasoned to taste
3 large hard-boiled eggs
salt and freshly ground pepper
6–8 anchovy fillets
1 small lemon
$\frac{1}{2}$ cup finely minced pickles
$\frac{1}{2}$ pound spinach, washed, trimmed, and shredded
$\frac{1}{2}$ pound sorrel, washed, trimmed, and shredded*
2 tablespoons finely minced garlic or shallots
optional: oil-and-vinegar dressing (recipe, p. 118)

1. Spread diced meat on the bottom of a large platter or salad bowl.
2. Separate yolks from whites of eggs. Grind yolks, then whites, in a mouli grater.
3. Sprinkle yolks, then whites, over meat. Dust lightly with salt and pepper. Place anchovies on top.
4. Squeeze out lemon juice over anchovies, or mince lemon pulp very finely and sprinkle over anchovies.
5. Top with pickles, spinach, sorrel, and garlic.
6. Serve with dressing on the side, if you wish.

SERVES 4

*When sorrel is not in season, you may replace it with an additional $\frac{1}{2}$ pound spinach.

121

To Pickle Red Cabbage

Take a Red Cabbage, chuse it a purple Red, for the light Red never proves a good Colour; so take your Cabbage, and shred it in thin Slices, season it with Pepper and Salt very well, let it lay all Night upon a broad Tin, or a Dripping pan; take a little Alegar, put to it a little Jamaica Pepper, and two or three Races of Ginger; boil them together, and when it is cold, pour it upon your Cabbage, and in two or three Days Time it will be fit for Use. You may throw a little Colliflower amongst it, and it will turn red.

Sarah Jackson, *The Director*

Pickled Red Cabbage. The newly available Jamaica pepper (allspice) was quickly taken up as a pickling spice, and with good results. *Alegar* (turned ale) was often used instead of vinegar (turned wine), since it was cheaper and very flavorful. The pickling solution below can be used with mushrooms, turnips, artichoke bottoms, or cauliflower, as the original recipe suggests. Very hard vegetables should be parboiled before they are soaked in the pickle.

Pickled cabbage goes nicely with hot or cold roast beef or pork.

1 small red cabbage
2 teaspoons salt
freshly ground pepper
$1\frac{1}{2}$ cups malt or wine vinegar
$\frac{1}{4}$ teaspoon allspice
4 thin slices ginger root

1. Discard outer leaves and hard central core of cabbage. Shred cabbage as you would for making cole slaw.
2. Spread out cabbage on a plate. Sprinkle with salt and pepper. Refrigerate overnight.
3. Drain off any accumulated water.
4. In a heavy enameled or stainless-steel saucepan, combine remaining ingredients.
5. Bring to a boil, then simmer for 15 minutes. Cool to room temperature.
6. Pack cabbage closely in an airtight container or a wide bottle with a tight-fitting lid.
7. Pour vinegar pickle over cabbage.
8. Shake container or bottle to coat all of the cabbage with vinegar pickle. Cool.
9. Refrigerate for 3 days before using. Turn container or bottle upside-down every 12 hours.
10. Remove ginger slices and adjust seasoning before serving.

NOTE: Pickled cabbage may be stored in the refrigerator up to 2 weeks.

CREATIVE ANACHRONISM: To make a variation of this recipe, you may add $\frac{1}{2}$ cup water and steam the pickled cabbage until it is soft.

An Incomparable Way to Make Mustard

Take a Quart of the best Mustard-seed you can get, let it be well dried, finely beat and sifted; then put to mixt it, two Parts white Wine Vinegar, and one Sack, also 1 Spoonful of double refin'd Sugar; stop it close, and 'twill keep a Year. If you are curious in your Seed, this way of making it gives a very agreeable Quickness and Flavour, that is not so disgusting in the Breath, as when Garlick is kept in the Jug.

The Complete Family Piece

Mustard. In *Acetaria,* John Evelyn specifies "that the Mustard (another noble Ingredient) be of the best Tewksberry; or else compos'd of the soundest and weightiest Yorkshire Seed, exquisitely sifted, winnow'd and freed from the Husks, . . . temper'd to the consistence of a Pap with Vinegar . . . from time to time made fresh."

I was surprised to discover how easy it is to make mustard with such "a very agreeable Quickness and Flavour."

124

$\frac{1}{2}$ cup yellow mustard seeds
$\frac{1}{2}$ cup white wine vinegar
$\frac{1}{4}$ cup dry sherry
2 teaspoons sugar

1. In a spice grinder or mortar and pestle, grind mustard seeds to a coarse powder. Sift out any large pieces of husk.
2. In a small bowl, combine vinegar, sherry, and sugar.
3. Stir in mustard powder.
4. Refrigerate in a bottle with a tight-fitting lid.

NOTE: Refrigerated, this mustard will keep for 4–6 months.

YIELD: 1 cup

125

To Stew Pasnips (S. Gr.)

Take sum pasnips & boyle them till thay are very soft, then scrape them clean & cutt them in thin slices, & put sum crame or good milk to them & put them on a cheafing dish of coles & let them stue a houre or two till thay are all to mash & prettey thick; stur it sumtimes & then put a good peice of buter in & a little salt, & sum sugar according to your tast, & sum grated nutmeg & a glass or two of white wine; stur all this together over the fire & put sum toasts of white bread in the dish & stru sum sugar over it.

Diana Astry, *Diana Astry's Recipe Book*

Stewed Parsnips. S. Gr., the cook who contributed this recipe to Diana Astry's collection, understood how to bring out the sweet and delicate taste of parsnips. The recipe specifically says to remove the skins after cooking. It may be that more of the flavor is retained when parsnips are boiled in their jackets, but I'm not sure that the difference is significant enough to warrant the nuisance of slipping off the softened skins. In other words, you may prefer to peel and slice the parsnips before boiling. Either way, this recipe will help you discover the subtleties of this fine vegetable.

1½ pounds small parsnips*
1 cup milk or heavy cream
3 tablespoons butter
3 tablespoons white wine
1 teaspoon sugar
pinch salt
freshly grated nutmeg
optional: toasted bread cubes
additional sugar

1. In a large pot, bring 3 quarts water to a rolling boil.
2. Cook parsnips about 20 minutes, or until they are easily pierced with a fork.
3. Drain. Slip off skins.
4. Mash parsnips. Add remaining ingredients except bread cubes and additional sugar.
5. Cook for 5 minutes over low heat.
6. Place bread cubes (if you are using them) in bowl. Pour parsnips over them. Sprinkle with sugar just before serving.

SERVES 6

*Judging by the long cooking time indicated in the original recipe, we can assume that the parsnips were extremely large. I prefer small parsnips, finding them sweeter and more delicate in flavor.

To Stew
Cabbidges

Take ye Cabidges & half boil ym then take ym out & not cruch them so put them into ye Stew Pan and Jamaka Pepper & a little mace pounded, put in two or 3 bay Leaves when half Stewd put in some Creame & 2 Anchovis when you take it up stir in some Butter.

In an Eighteenth Century Kitchen

Cabbage with Anchovy-Cream Sauce. I have always liked cabbage, but I never knew it could taste this good. The strong taste cabbage sometimes has is removed in the parboiling, and we are left with a very delicate vegetable which responds beautifully to the cream sauce.

1 small cabbage
1 cup heavy cream
1 bay leaf
generous $\frac{1}{4}$ teaspoon allspice
pinch mace
3 anchovy fillets, chopped
1 tablespoon butter
salt

1. In a large pot, bring 3 quarts water to a rolling boil.
2. Wash cabbage and quarter it, removing hard central core.
3. Cook cabbage for 3 minutes. Drain.
4. In a bowl, combine cream, bay leaf, allspice, mace, and anchovies.
5. Place cabbage in a heavy pot. Pour cream sauce over cabbage.
6. Cover and cook over very low heat about 10 minutes, or until cabbage is soft but still somewhat crunchy. (Since cream sauce burns easily, you may wish to place the pot on a flame tamer, or continue the cooking process in a moderate [350°F] oven. In any case, watch the pot closely during this stage.)
7. Discard bay leaf. Set cabbage on a serving platter.
8. Stir butter into sauce. Check seasoning and spoon sauce over cabbage.

SERVES 4

Fry'd Sellery

You must first boil it half enough, then let it cool, and make a Batter with a little Rhenish Wine, the Yolks of Eggs with a little Flower and Salt: Dip every Head in, and fry them with clarify'd Butter, and sauce them with melted Butter.

Charles Carter, *The Compleat City and Country Cook*

1 small bunch of celery,
    washed
$\frac{1}{2}$ cup flour
$\frac{1}{8}$ teaspoon salt
yolk of 1 large egg
$\frac{1}{2}$ cup white wine
equal parts clarified butter and light oil for shallow frying

Fried Celery. This is an unusual and easy way to prepare celery. The crisp bits make a fine side dish at dinner, and a very suitable hors d'oeuvre.

1. In a large pot, bring 3 quarts salted water to a rolling boil.
2. Cut celery stalks into 2-inch lengths. Boil them for 5 minutes.
3. Drain in a colander. Refresh under cold water. Drain, then pat thoroughly dry.
4. In a bowl, prepare batter by combining flour, salt, egg yolk, and wine.
5. In a heavy skillet, slowly heat butter and oil. When fat is sufficiently hot, a small bread cube will brown in 60 seconds.
6. Dip each piece of celery into batter, then drop it into hot fat. Fry until both sides are golden. Do not fry more than 3–4 pieces at a time. Drain on paper towels.
7. Keep hot in a 200°F oven until ready to serve.

SERVES 4–6

OF GOOD GRAVY,
A CULLIS, AND
A RAGOO

To Make Good Gravy

Take a lean Piece of Beef, cut in thin Slices well beaten, and fry'd brown with a Lumb of Butter, till the Goodness is out, then throw the Meat away, and put into the gravy a Quart of strong Broth, and half a Pint of Claret, four Anchovies, a Shalot, a little Lemon-Peel, Cloves, Mace, Pepper and Salt; let all boil well together; and when your Gravy is ready, put it into a gally-pot, and set it by till call'd for.

Robert Smith, *Court Cookery*

Good Gravy. Good gravy was essential and used frequently, much as we use strong stock today, as a base for soups and sauces. This particular gravy is very flavorful, and I strongly recommend using it in those recipes that call for gravy. For suggestions on storing extra gravy, see p. 54.

132

2 tablespoons butter
$\frac{1}{2}$ pound chuck, sliced thin, pounded, and chopped*
4 cups strong beef broth
1 cup claret
8 anchovy fillets, chopped
1 large shallot, minced
1 teaspoon finely minced lemon peel
$\frac{1}{8}$ teaspoon cloves
generous pinch mace
salt and freshly ground pepper

1. In a large soup pot, melt butter.
2. Fry meat over low heat until it is brown on both sides.
3. Add remaining ingredients to pot. Bring to a boil, then reduce heat and simmer for 30 minutes.
4. Check seasoning.
5. Pass gravy through a strainer into a bottle with a tight-fitting lid. Store for use.

NOTE: This gravy can be stored in the refrigerator up to 5 days, or in the freezer for 1–2 months.

YIELD: about 5 cups

*You may eliminate the butter and meat and proceed directly to step 3. While the meat flavor enriches the taste of the gravy considerably, if your broth is tasty you may not think it worth the additional cost.

133

A Ragoo of Asparagus

Scrape a hundred of Grass very clean, and throw it into cold Water. When you have scraped and picked, cut it very small, a young Lettice clean washed, and cut small, a large Onion peeled, and cut small, put a quarter of a pound of Butter into a Stew-pan. When it is melted, throw in the above Things: Toss them about, and fry them ten Minutes; then season them with a little Pepper and Salt, shake in a little Flour, toss them about, then pour in half a Pint of Gravy. Let them stew, till the Sauce is very thick and good; then pour all into your Dish. Save a few of the little Tops of the Grass to garnish the Dish.

Hannah Glasse, *The Art of Cookery*

Asparagus Ragout. Made with fresh young "grass," this *ragoo* is exquisite. You may use it as a sauce for flounder pie (recipe, p. 92) or roasted fowl, and it would also make a fine vegetable side dish. For an elegant soup, thin it with chicken broth and serve hot or cold.

134

1 pound thin asparagus
4 tablespoons butter
1 cup finely shredded lettuce
$\frac{1}{2}$ cup finely chopped onion
1 teaspoon flour
$\frac{1}{2}$ cup gravy (recipe, p. 132)
salt and freshly ground pepper

1. Wash asparagus. Snap off the tough bottom ends and dice asparagus finely, leaving 5–6 tips whole.
2. In a saucepan, melt butter. Add diced asparagus and whole tips, lettuce, and onion.
3. Toss to coat vegetables in butter. Sauté for 10 minutes, stirring occasionally.
4. Stir in flour.
5. Add gravy and salt and pepper to taste. Simmer until asparagus is tender.
6. Serve in a sauceboat with whole asparagus tips arranged on top.

YIELD: 2 cups

A Very Good Cullis

Take Carrots and Parsnips, with a few Roots of Parsley; cut them in Slices, toss them up in a Stew-pan with some Butter or Water; then pound them in a Mortar, with some blanched Almonds and the Crumb of a French Roll soaked in Broth; boil all these together, and season it as usual; strain it through a Sieve, and use it as you find Occasion.

John Middleton, *Five Hundred New Receipts*

Carrot-Almond Cullis. Since most *cullises* were rich broths made of meat, this recipe is rather unusual. I have added very little broth, and the result is a thick and pudding-like *cullis* which may be used to thicken soups and sauces, or served as a vegetable side dish. By adding more broth, you will have a delicious gravy or a fine soup.

4 tablespoons butter

$1\frac{1}{2}$ pounds combination of carrots, parsnips, and parsley root, trimmed, peeled, and thinly sliced

$\frac{1}{4}$ cup bread crumbs

$\frac{1}{2}$ cup (or more) chicken broth

$\frac{1}{4}$ cup blanched almonds, finely ground

salt and freshly ground pepper (preferably white)

1. In a large heavy pot with a tight-fitting cover, melt butter.
2. Add vegetables. Toss until they are well coated with butter.
3. Cover pot and cook over low heat about 45 minutes, or until vegetables are soft.
4. Purée vegetables in a blender or pass them through the fine blade of a food mill.
5. Soak bread crumbs in chicken broth.
6. Add bread crumbs and almonds to vegetable purée.
7. Pass mixture through a large-meshed strainer, if you wish. (The purée will already be quite smooth.)
8. Reheat. Check seasoning.

YIELD: $2\frac{1}{2}$ cups

138

OF BISCUITS, PUFFS, CAKES, TARTS, AND A TANSEY

To Make Biscuits of Red Beet-Roots, Call'd the Crimson Biscuit

Take the roots of Red-Beets, and boil them tender; clean them, and beat them in a Mortar with as much Sugar, finely sifted; some Butter; the Yolks of hard Eggs, a little Flower; some Spice, finely beaten, and some Orange-Flower-Water, and a little Lemon-Juice. When they are well mix'd, and reduced to a Paste, make them into Cakes, and dry them in a slow Oven.

R. Bradley, *The Country Housewife and Lady's Director*

Crimson Biscuits. It's fun asking your guests what gives these biscuits such a beautiful color. It usually takes quite a few hints before someone will think of beets. It wasn't until the nineteenth century that beet sugar was commercially produced, but cooks in the eighteenth century clearly recognized the sweetness of this vegetable.

$\frac{1}{2}$ pound beets
$\frac{1}{4}$ cup butter at room temperature
yolks of 2 large hard-boiled eggs

½ cup sugar

1 teaspoon lemon juice

1 teaspoon orange-flower water

1½ cups flour

scant ⅛ teaspoon cloves

1. In a pot, bring 2 quarts water to a rolling boil.
2. Cut tops from beets, leaving 1 inch of stem. Wash beets.
3. Cook beets until they are tender. (Allow ½ to 1 hour for small beets.)
4. Drain beets, then slip off skins and trim off stems.
5. Pass beets through the fine blade of a food mill or purée in a blender. You should have about ½ cup of purée.
6. In a large bowl, cream butter and egg yolks.
7. Beat in sugar.
8. Stir lemon juice and orange-flower water into beet purée. Blend thoroughly with creamed butter.
9. Sift in flour and cloves. Stir with a fork, then knead dough gently just until flour is absorbed.
10. On a lightly floured board, roll out dough to ¼-inch thickness. (If dough is sticky, chill before rolling.)
11. Cut out 2-inch rounds or shapes of your choice. Brush off excess flour.
12. Bake on a greased baking sheet at 275°F for 15 minutes, or until bottoms are pale orange around the edges.
13. Cool on a rack. Store in an airtight tin.

YIELD: 1½ dozen biscuits

141

To Make
Naples Bisket

Take 3 Egs both Yolkes & Whites, & beat them in a bason, or wooden Bowle a quarter of an hour, then put to them halfe a pound of Sugar, & beat them together as longe againe, then put to them 6 Ounces of fine flower & a graine or 2 of muske, being Steeped in a Spoonfull or two of Rosewater, & beat them well together while your Oven is a heating, & when it is as hot as for Manchett, butter your pans, & put your bread into them & backe it, & dry it, & keep it for your Use.

In an Eighteenth Century Kitchen

Naples Biscuit. This *bisket* is initially prepared like a sponge cake, and the rising power of well-beaten eggs is quite dramatic to behold. The crumbs of *Naples bisket,* thoroughly dried in the oven, were used as thickeners and binders in many eighteenth-century recipes. Real musk is no longer readily available, so I've substituted the seeds as a rough approximation. It will not harm the end product in any way to leave them out.

optional: 12 musk seeds

2 tablespoons rose water

3 large eggs at room temperature

1 cup sugar

$1\frac{1}{3}$ cups flour

1. Grind musk seeds with a mortar and pestle. Steep them in rose water for 1 hour.

2. With an electric beater, beat eggs for 5 minutes. Add rose-water–musk solution (or plain rose water).

3. Add sugar gradually and continue beating for an additional 5 minutes.

4. Sift in flour, beating all the while.

5. Bake in a 9- by $3\frac{1}{2}$-inch greased tube pan with removable bottom or sides at 350°F about 40 minutes. When done, a toothpick inserted into the cake should come out dry.

6. Remove cake from pan. Cool on rack.

NOTE: I usually freeze half this cake to be used as needed for the sponge base of Westminster fool (recipe, p. 170). The other half I cut into $\frac{1}{2}$-inch slices and dry on a baking sheet at 250°F, then grate into crumbs for use in other recipes (pp. 65, 95, 150). Crumbs should be stored in an airtight container.

YIELD : 8 slices for Westminster fool plus about $1\frac{1}{2}$ cups biscuit crumbs

To Make Little Round Ratafea-Puffs

Take half a Pound of Kernels, or Bitter-Almonds, beat very stiff, and a Pound and a Half of Sifted Sugar; make it up to a stiff Paste with White of Eggs whipt to a Froth; beat it well in a Mortar, and make it up in little Loaves; then bake 'em in a very cool Oven, on Paper and Tin-Plates.

Mrs. Mary Eales's Receipts

Ratafia Puffs. Ratafia, the flavor of ground apricot kernels or bitter almonds, was much favored during the eighteenth century. Since the kernels are no longer sold, I have added a drop of sweet almond extract to flavor these little meringues. As a result, they take on the taste we normally associate with marzipan, but their texture is crisp and they are beautifully white with just a touch of golden brown on top.

144

1½ cups (½ pound) blanched almonds
2 cups sugar
scant ¼ teaspoon almond extract
5 egg whites

1. Grind almonds in a mouli grater or blender. (If you use a blender, grind them together with some of the sugar.) Combine sugar (or remaining sugar) with ground almonds.
2. Stir almond extract into egg whites. Beat until stiff.
3. Fold in almond-sugar mixture.
4. Cover a baking sheet with baking parchment. Drop teaspoonfuls of batter onto parchment, leaving 1½ inches between each.
5. Bake at 300°F for 30 minutes, or until puffs are golden around the edges.
6. Lift parchment from baking sheet and place it on a rack.
7. When puffs are cool, gently remove from parchment with a spatula.
8. Store in an airtight tin.

NOTE: If you cannot locate baking parchment, you may wish to bake the puffs on edible rice paper. If you do, simply tear off excess paper around each puff after the puffs have cooled.

YIELD: 3 dozen puffs

Shrewsbury Cakes

a pund and half of flouer, half a pund of sugar, half a nutmeg some beaten cinnamon the sugar and spice must be sifted into the flouer. wet it with two eggs, and as much melted butter as will make it of a good stifness, mould it well and roll it out what shape you please.

Recipes from a Ladies Diary

Shrewsbury Cakes. Here are some crisp, delicately spiced butter cookies which I like to serve with strawberry fool, syllabub, or buttered oranges (recipes, pp. 172, 178, 168).

$2\frac{1}{2}$ cups flour
$\frac{1}{2}$ cup sugar
$\frac{1}{4}$ teaspoon freshly grated nutmeg
$\frac{1}{2}$ teaspoon cinnamon
1 large egg, beaten
$\frac{1}{2}$ pound butter, melted and cooled to room temperature

1. Sift flour, sugar, and spices into a large bowl.
2. Add egg and butter, stirring with a fork.
3. Place mixture on a floured board. Knead dough gently just until flour is absorbed. Roll or press dough to $\frac{1}{4}$-inch thickness. (Do not be concerned if dough is a bit crumbly.)
4. Cut out 2-inch rounds or "cakes" of whatever shape you please.
5. Transfer "cakes" to a well-greased baking sheet. (A spatula simplifies this task.)
6. Bake at 350°F for 12–15 minutes, or until bottoms are a delicate golden brown.
7. Transfer "cakes" to a rack to cool.
8. Store in an airtight tin.

YIELD: about 2 dozen "cakes"

To Make a Tart of the Ananas, or Pine-Apple

Take a Pine-Apple, and twist off its crown: then pare it free from the Knots, and cut it in slices about half an Inch thick; then stew it with a little Canary Wine, or Madera Wine, and some Sugar, till it is thoroughly hot, and it will distribute its Flavour to the Wine.much better than anything we can add to it. When it is as one would have it, take it from the Fire; and when it is cool, put it into a sweet paste with its Liquor, and bake it gently, a little while, and when it comes from the Oven, pour Cream over it (if you have it) and serve it either hot or cold.

R. Bradley, *The Country Housewife and Lady's Director*

Pineapple Tart. This pie is sensational, especially when made with an almond pastry shell (recipe, p. 166).

9-inch unbaked pie pastry shell
1 large ripe pineapple
$\frac{1}{2}$ cup sweet Madeira or sherry
1 tablespoon sugar
optional: heavy cream

1. Prebake pastry shell, covered with aluminum foil and filled with beans, at 375°F for 15 minutes. Remove beans and foil. Bake for an additional 5 minutes. Set aside.
2. Remove pineapple crown. Cut pineapple into slices $\frac{1}{2}$ inch thick.
3. With an apple corer and knife, cut away skin and knots around edges and remove central hard core.
4. In a bowl, marinate pineapple slices in wine for 2 hours, turning occasionally.
5. Place pineapple slices and wine in a pot. Cook, covered, for 20 minutes, turning slices over after 10 minutes. Drain slices but reserve liquid.
6. Arrange slices attractively, overlapping each other, in pastry shell.
7. Make a glaze by boiling wine with sugar until reduced to $\frac{1}{4}$ cup.
8. Paint glaze on pineapple slices.
9. Bake at 300°F for 20 minutes.
10. Serve warm or cold with a small pitcher of cream.

SERVES 8

149

To Make Chocolate Tarts

Take 4 Ounces of Chocolate grated small, put to it a pint of Cream, 2 or 3 spoonfulls of Orange flower water, one spoonfull of sugar, ye yolk of 6 Eggs and half a pint of new milk; four spoonfulls of white wine, stir all together over a clear fire till thick, then take it up and let it cool, then add ye juice of an orange and ye yolk of 2 Eggs stir'd together and put it in your pasty pan or dish first cover'd with past, bake it without a Cover only making a handsom border or garniture of past round it, when baked scrape loaf sugar over and serve it: do not forget to put in either ye crumb of a Roll or a Naples biskett grated.

Daniel Moult, *Manuscript Cookery Book*

Chocolate Tart. Chocolate came from the New World, and, like coffee, was used primarily as a drink in the late seventeenth century and after. This recipe is the successful result of experimentation to find new uses for chocolate. It's hard to eat this tart slowly enough; there are so many levels of flavor to be appreciated.

150

8-inch unbaked pie (or tart) pastry shell
3 ounces bittersweet chocolate, grated
1 cup heavy cream
$\frac{1}{2}$ cup milk
$1\frac{1}{2}$ teaspoons orange-flower water
1 teaspoon (or more) sugar
yolks of 3 large eggs, beaten
2 tablespoons dry white wine
optional: 2 tablespoons Naples biscuit crumbs (recipe p. 142)
2–3 tablespoons orange juice
1 additional egg yolk, beaten

1. Prebake pastry shell, covered with aluminum foil and filled with beans, at 375°F for 10 minutes. Remove beans and foil. Bake for an additional 5 minutes. Set aside.
2. In the top of a double boiler, combine all ingredients except biscuit crumbs, orange juice, and additional egg yolk.
3. Set pot into hot but not boiling water. Cook over medium heat, whisking frequently, until custard begins to thicken.
4. Remove from heat. Stir in biscuit crumbs (if you are using them), orange juice, and additional egg yolk.
5. Pour into pastry shell.
6. Bake at 375°F for 40 minutes, or until custard is set.
7. Cool to room temperature. Chill before serving.

SERVES 6–8

To Make Prune Tarts

Take a Pound and a half of Prunes, stew them in Claret, and when they are tender strain them through a thin Strainer, rubbing them to pieces with your Hands; pour some of the Liquor they were stewed in into a Strainer, to wash the Prunes from the Stones, so that nothing but the Stones and Skins remain in the Strainer, set your Dish with the Pulp of the Prunes on a Chafing-Dish of Coals, with some whole Cinnamon, large Mace, candied Orange Peel and Citron minced; season it with Sugar and Rose-water; let it boil up 'till it is thick; then take out your whole Spice, and having raised your Tarts, harden the Crusts of them in the Oven; then fill your Tarts and lid them, they will require but very little baking; when they are done, and you have dished them, strew over them fine Sugar.

John Middleton, *Five Hundred New Receipts*

Prune Tarts.

Unless some Sweetness at the Bottom lye,
Who cares for all the crinkling of the Pye?

William King, author of this couplet from *The Art of Cookery in Imitation of Horace's Art of Poetry* (1730), would not have found this prune tart disappointing.

152

8-inch unbaked pie pastry shell and pastry for lid
3 cups (1$\frac{1}{4}$ pounds) pitted prunes
1$\frac{1}{4}$ cups claret
$\frac{1}{2}$ cup chopped candied orange peel
$\frac{1}{2}$ cup chopped candied citron
$\frac{1}{4}$ teaspoon cinnamon
$\frac{1}{8}$ teaspoon mace
1 tablespoon rose water
1 tablespoon confectioners' sugar

1. Prebake pastry shell, covered with aluminum foil and filled with beans, at 375°F for 10 minutes. Remove beans and foil. Bake for an additional 5 minutes. Set aside.
2. Meanwhile, cook prunes in claret about 15 minutes, or until they are very soft.
3. Pass prunes and claret through the medium blade of a food mill or purée in a blender.
4. Combine prune purée with remaining ingredients except sugar. Pour into pie shell.
5. Cover filling with pastry lid. Slash lid decoratively in a few places to allow steam to escape.
6. Bake at 375°F for 30 minutes, or until lid is golden brown.
7. Dust lightly with confectioners' sugar. Serve warm or room temperature.

SERVES 8

To Make Apple Tansey

Take three Pippins, slice them round in thin slices, and fry them with butter, then beat four Eggs, with six spoonfuls of Cream, a little Rose-water, nutmeg, and Sugar, and stir them together, and pour it over the Apples: Let it fry a little, and turn it with a Pye-plate. Garnish with lemon and Sugar strewed over it.

Eliza Smith, *The Compleat Housewife*

Apple Omelet. The original *tansies* were egg-based puddings or pancakes flavored and colored green with the herb tansy. But by the eighteenth century, the term was used more loosely, and came to be synonymous with an omelet, herbs or not.

This sweet *tansey* would make a nice luncheon entrée or dinner dessert.

2 tablespoons sweet butter
2 large apples, peeled, cored, and thinly sliced
4 large eggs
2 tablespoons light cream or milk
1 tablespoon rose water
1 teaspoon sugar
freshly grated nutmeg
topping: juice of $\frac{1}{2}$ small lemon, confectioners' sugar

1. In a large omelet pan, melt butter.
2. Cook apple slices over low heat, stirring occasionally, until they are soft but firm.
3. In a bowl, beat eggs until frothy. Blend in cream, rose water, sugar, and nutmeg.
4. Pour egg mixture over apples and cook over high heat, sliding pan firmly back and forth so omelet doesn't stick. Lower heat, and cook gently until eggs are just short of firm.
5. Flip omelet over to brown the other side, or brown the top under the broiler.
6. Sprinkle with lemon juice and confectioners' sugar. Serve immediately.

SERVES 2

155

To Make a Good Seed Cake

Take a Quarter of a Peck of Flour, two Pounds of Butter beaten to a Cream, a Pound and three quarters of fine Sugar, one Ounce of Carraway-seeds, three Ounces of candy'd Orange-Peel and Citron, ten Eggs, half the whites only, a little Rose Water, a glass of Sack, a little new Yeast, and half a Pint of Cream, mix it up and lay it by the Fire to rise; then bake it in a Hoop, and butter your Paper: when it is baked, ice it over with Whites of Eggs and Sugar, and set it in again to harden.

The Country Magazine

Seed Cake. Of all historical recipes, those for baked goods are the most difficult to make, primarily because the quality of yeast and flour have changed significantly over the years. Also, one can't taste and make additions along the way; once the dough is in the oven, its fate is sealed.

I failed in my early attempts to give this enriched cake a pleasing texture, but since the recipe is so typical of the period, I felt it worth repeated efforts. I am now enjoying seed cake every morning, toasted, for breakfast.

Caraway seeds are thought to keep lovers from proving fickle, and it is a known fact that tame pigeons, if given a piece of seed cake, will never stray from their dovecote.

156

1 cup flour
2 tablespoons sugar
$\frac{1}{2}$ ounce (2 packages) active dry yeast
$\frac{1}{2}$ cup warm milk
2 large eggs plus 1 yolk
2 tablespoons rose water
2 tablespoons dry sherry
6 ounces butter, melted and cooled to room temperature
additional $2\frac{1}{4}$ cups flour
additional $\frac{1}{2}$ cup sugar
1 tablespoon caraway seeds
$\frac{3}{4}$ cup mixed candied orange peel and citron, coarsely chopped

FOR ICING:

1 egg white

1 tablespoon confectioners' sugar

1. Sift 1 cup flour and 2 tablespoons sugar into a large bowl.
2. Dissolve yeast in warm milk. Pour into flour. With a wooden spoon, mix until smooth.
3. Cover bowl with a clean cloth and leave in a warm place for 20 minutes. Batter will become frothy. (If batter doesn't expand, chances are your yeast has expired, and you had better begin again with new yeast.)
4. Meanwhile, in another bowl, beat eggs with rose water and sherry.

5. When batter is frothy, add egg mixture and butter.

6. Sift in additional flour and sugar. Add caraway seeds and candied fruit.

7. Spoon knead this mixture: Sit down and place bowl between your knees. Then, holding a long-handled wooden spoon with both hands, stir vigorously 100 times. (Since dough is thick, this is hard work.)

8. Cover bowl with a cloth and set in a warm place for 2 hours, or until dough is doubled in bulk.

9. Spoon knead 40 times.

10. Pour dough into a very well greased 9- by $2\frac{1}{2}$-inch tube pan or savarin ring. Cover with a cloth and set in a warm place for 1 additional hour.

11. Bake at 425°F for 10 minutes. Then reduce temperature to 375°F and bake for an additional 35 minutes. Cake is done when a toothpick inserted into the center comes out dry. Turn cake out of pan onto a baking sheet or an ovenproof platter.

12. Whip egg white and confectioners' sugar to form soft peaks. Paint icing on cake and return to oven for 5 minutes, or until golden brown.

13. Cool cake on a rack.

SERVES 8–10

OF PASTES, FOOLS, CONFECTIONS, AND A WHIPP'D SYLLABUB

Hot Paste for Minced Pyes

You may also make an hot Paste, for minced Pyes, or such like, by taking a quantity of Flour as you like, and breaking a Pound or two of Butter into a large Sauce-pan of Water; and when the Butter is melted, make an hollow in the midst of the Flour and scumming off the Butter, throw it, at times, into the Flour, with some of the boiling hot Water along with it; then, when you have enough for your use, work it into a stiff Paste, and lay it before the Fire, cover'd with a Cloth, and cut off such bits as you want, just when you are going to use them. This Paste does very well for raised Pyes. Some will make this Paste by breaking in a Pound of Butter into a quarter of a Peck of Flour, and then pouring on it some scalding hot Water, enough to work it to a stiff Paste.

R. Bradley, *The Country Housewife and Lady's Director*

Hot-Water Pie Pastry.

Poets and Pastry Cooks will be the same,
Since both of them their Images must frame.
Chimaera's from the Poet's fancy flow,
The Cook contrives his Shapes in real Dough.

William King, in *The Art of Cookery . . . ,* is referring to the eighteenth-century custom of making pies in fanciful shapes. "Raising a crust" is an acquired skill considerably simplified if you own a wooden pie mold or have taken a course in hand-built pottery. The solutions offered in the recipe for preparing mincemeat pie (p. 94) with hot-water pastry seem sensible and are not nearly so risky.

$\frac{1}{2}$ pound butter
$\frac{1}{2}$ cup water
4 cups flour
1 teaspoon salt
optional: scant tablespoon sugar (use only with sweet fillings)

1. In a small saucepan, heat butter and water and bring to a boil. Stir until butter dissolves.
2. In a large bowl, mix flour, salt, and sugar (if you are using it).
3. Slowly pour boiling liquid into dry ingredients, stirring all the while with a fork.
4. Knead dough for a few moments, until it is firm.
5. Cut off about one third of the dough for a lid. Wrap in a towel and set in a warm place.
6. Roll out remaining dough to desired shape about $\frac{1}{2}$ inch thick.
7. As soon as possible, roll out lid to desired shape.

NOTE: This dough, unlike other pastry doughs, is meant to be rolled and shaped when warm; it becomes stiff and brittle when cool. So prepare it just before you are ready to line your baking dish.

YIELD : dough for lining and lid of a $1\frac{1}{2}$-quart raised pie mold or 9- by 5- by 3-inch loaf pan

A Good Paste for Tarts

Take a Pint of Flour, and rub a Quarter of a Pound of Butter into it, beat two Eggs, with a Spoonful of double-refin'd Sugar, and two or three Spoonsfulls of Cream to make it into Paste; work it as little as you can; roll it out thin; butter your Tins, dust on some Flour, then lay in your Paste, and do not fill them too full.

Sarah Jackson, *The Director*

Crisp Pastry for Tarts. This recipe, using eggs as the primary liquid ingredient, is quite typical of the period. It creates a stiff crust and is particularly nice with moist fillings.

$2\frac{1}{4}$ cups flour
1 tablespoon sugar or 1 teaspoon salt*
$\frac{1}{4}$ pound cold butter, cut into bits
2 large eggs, beaten
heavy cream or milk
additional butter
additional flour

*For a sweet pie, use sugar; for a savory pie, use salt.

1. In a large bowl, combine flour and sugar or salt.
2. Cut in ¼ pound butter until mixture has the consistency of coarse meal.
3. Place eggs in a measuring cup. Add enough cream to make ⅓ cup.
4. Work liquid into flour, using fingertips or a pastry blender, until dough forms a firm ball.
5. Divide dough into 2 equal balls. Wrap in waxed paper.
6. Chill for 1 hour before rolling.
7. Lightly grease and flour pie tins before lining them with dough.

NOTE: This pastry, raw or prebaked, may be refrigerated for a few days or frozen until needed.

YIELD: two 9-inch pastry shells

163

A Sweet Paste

If you would have a sweet Paste; then take half a Pound of
Butter, and rub it into about a Pound of Flour, with two or
three Ounces of Double-refined Sugar powder'd, and make it a
Paste, with cold Milk, some Sack and Brandy. This is a very good
one.

R. Bradley, *The Country Housewife and Lady's Director*

Sweet Pastry. Sweet it is, and very tasty, too.

¹⁄₂ pound cold butter, cut into bits
2³⁄₄ cups flour
¹⁄₄ cup sugar
2 tablespoons cold milk
2 tablespoons chilled sherry
2 tablespoons chilled brandy

1. Place butter in a large bowl.
2. Sift flour and sugar onto butter.
3. Rub butter into dry ingredients with fingertips or a pastry blender until mixture resembles coarse meal.
4. Combine milk, sherry, and brandy.
5. Work in liquid with fingertips or a pastry blender until dough forms a firm ball.
6. Divide dough into 2 equal balls. Wrap in waxed paper.
7. Chill for 1 hour before rolling.

NOTE: This pastry, raw or prebaked, may be refrigerated for a few days or frozen until needed.

YIELD: two 9-inch pastry shells

Almond Paste

Take a Pound of Almonds and blanch them and beat them in a Mortar very fine; put some Water to them to keep them from oil; then mix up your Almonds with two Pounds of Flower, rubbing it well in with one Pound of Powder'd sugar; then put in half a Pound of Butter and six yolks of Eggs, with two Whites; this Paste will serve for rich Tarts or Sweet Pyes; it will soon bake.

Charles Carter, *The Compleat City and Country Cook*

Almond Pastry. Ground nuts in pie pastry make a crisp shell which provides welcome contrast to smooth fillings. I particularly like to use this crust for making chocolate tarts (recipe, p. 150).

$^3/_4$ cup ($^1/_4$ pound) blanched almonds
ice water
$1^1/_2$ cups flour
$^1/_2$ cup sugar
4 tablespoons butter, cut into small bits
1 large egg, beaten
additional ice water

1. Grind almonds in a mortar and pestle or a blender, adding 2 tablespoons ice water to prevent them from turning into a paste.
2. In a bowl, mix ground almonds, flour, and sugar.
3. Rub or cut in butter.
4. Add egg. Knead dough into a ball, adding a few tablespoons of ice water if needed to create a firm dough.
5. Divide dough into 2 equal balls. If you wish to roll it out, first chill thoroughly. Otherwise, simply press dough into a pie plate.

NOTE: This crust, raw or prebaked, may be refrigerated for a few days or frozen until needed. If using almond pastry for a top crust, crimp edges by pressing dough firmly to rim of pie plate with the tines of a fork.

YIELD: two 9-inch pastry shells

Buttered Oranges

Rasp the peel of four oranges into a pint of water; to which add a pint of Orange juice and the yolks of twelve eggs and the whites but of 4, putting as much sugar as will sweeten to your palate, strain it, set it on the fire, and when it is pretty well thickened, put in a piece of butter as big as a couple of nuts, and keep stirring it till it is cold.

N. Bailey, *Dictionarium Domesticum*

Buttered Oranges. If clouds were orange and could be eaten, this is what they'd taste like.

3 large juice oranges
2 large eggs plus 4 yolks, beaten
2–3 tablespoons sugar
2 tablespoons sweet butter, cut into bits

1. Finely grate rinds of oranges. Be careful not to grate the white pith beneath the rind, as it is bitter. Set aside.
2. Squeeze oranges until you have 1 cup juice.
3. Combine orange juice, eggs, and sugar to taste. (The amount of sugar depends on the sweetness of the juice.)
4. Pour mixture through a fine-meshed strainer into the top of a double boiler. Stir in grated rind.
5. Set pot into hot but not boiling water.
6. Cook over moderate heat, whisking, until custard thickens. When whisk makes ribbons on the surface, remove from heat. Place pot in a large bowl of cold water.
7. Whisk in butter, one bit at a time, until it melts.
8. Spoon small portions of custard into four sherry or wine glasses.
9. Chill before serving.

SERVES 4

Westminster-Fool

Take a Penny-loaf, cut it into thin Slices, wet them with Sack, lay them in the Bottom of a Dish, take a Quart of Cream, beat up six Eggs, two Spoonfuls of Rose-Water, a Blade of Mace, Some grated Nutmeg, sweeten to your Taste. Put this all into a Sauce-pan, and keep stirring all the time over a slow Fire for fear of curdling. When it begins to be thick, pour it into the Dish over the Bread; let it stand till it is cold, and serve it up.

Hannah Glasse, *The Art of Cookery*

Westminster Fool. This recipe resembles the contemporary English trifle, but in the eighteenth century a trifle was a dish of junket, and in the nineteenth century trifle was often a fruit cream.

Call it what they will, this is a dessert full of characteristic eighteenth-century flavors: sherry, rose water, nutmeg, and custard.

6-8 slices Naples biscuit (recipe, p. 142) or plain pound cake*
$\frac{1}{3}$ cup sweet sherry
2 cups heavy cream
3 large eggs, beaten
$\frac{1}{4}$ cup sugar
$1\frac{1}{2}$ teaspoons rose water
scant $\frac{1}{8}$ teaspoon freshly grated nutmeg
generous pinch mace

1. Place biscuit slices side by side in a large deep dish. Moisten with sherry. Set aside.
2. In the top of a double boiler, combine remaining ingredients.
3. Set over hot but not boiling water and cook, stirring constantly, until custard is thick enough to coat the back of a spoon. If custard begins to boil, remove it from heat immediately or it will curdle.
4. Remove custard from heat. Stir as it begins to cool, in order to release excess moisture.
5. Pour over biscuit slices. Serve warm or chilled.

NOTE: Westminster fool is rather white-looking, so plan to serve it in a colorful dish or consider a decorative garnish of crystalized flowers.

SERVES 6-8

*The "Penny-loaf" in the original recipe would have been made of fine-quality white flour, and you may wish to use slices of white bread for the base. Recipes similar to this one call for Naples biscuit; I prefer the taste and texture of the latter, or of pound cake.

171

To Make Strawberry or Raspberry Fool

Take a pint of Raspberries, squeeze and strain the Juice with Orange flower water; put to the Juice five ounces of fine Sugar; then set a pint of Cream over the Fire, and let it boil up; then put in the Juice, give it one stir round, and then put it into your Bason; stir it a little in the Bason, and when 'tis cold use it.

Eliza Smith, *The Compleat Housewife*

Strawberry Fool. Elizabeth David, in her pamphlet *Syllabubs and Fruit Fools,* suggests that "the French word *foulé,* meaning crushed or pressed, must surely have some bearing on the English name." Fools in the eighteenth century were often made by combining crushed fruit with boiled cream, as in the recipe below, but the term was also applied to flavored custards (recipe, p. 170).

1 pint strawberries (or raspberries)
1 cup heavy cream
approximately 2 tablespoons sugar
scant ½ teaspoon orange-flower water

1. If using strawberries, remove stems. Wash fruit.
2. In a blender, purée fruit to a thick liquid. Pass purée through a strainer with the back of a spoon.
3. In a pot, bring cream to a boil.
4. Stir in fruit purée. Sweeten to taste with sugar. (The amount of sugar depends on the sweetness of the fruit.)
5. Remove from heat. Stir in orange-flower water.
6. Pour into long-stemmed wine goblets or small parfait glasses.
7. Chill before serving.

SERVES 4

Marmalet of Oranges

Pare your Oranges as thin as possible, then boil them 'till they are soft; then take double the Number of good Pippins, cut them into Halves, core them, and boil them to Pap, so as they may not lose their Colour; strain the Pulp, and add a Pound of Sugar to every Pint: Afterwards take out the Orange-Pulp, cut the Peel, and let it be made very soft by boiling, in order to be bruised in the Juice of Lemons, and boiled up again to a Consistence with your Apple-Pulp, and one half a Pint of Rose-Water.

The Whole Duty of a Woman

Orange Marmalade. It was common during this period to make marmalade by combining citrus rind with apple jelly, and it's quite a fine idea. In fact, this preserve is so special that I recommend bottling some for house gifts.

1 pound juice oranges
2 pounds cooking apples
2 cups sugar
juice of $\frac{1}{2}$ small lemon
1 tablespoon (or more) rose water

174

1. Scrub oranges. Slice thinly and discard seeds.
2. In a large, heavy enameled or stainless-steel pot, soak oranges in water to cover for 12 hours.
3. Bring water to a boil. Reduce heat and simmer for 40 minutes.
4. Remove from heat. Cover and let stand for another 12 hours.
5. Return to a boil. Reduce heat and simmer until peels are very soft and easy to chew. Drain peels and pulp, chop them coarsely, and set aside.
6. Core and quarter apples. In a large pot over moderate heat, cook them in water to cover until they are puffy and very soft. Drain and let them cool slightly.
7. Place some cooked apple in a jelly bag* and squeeze until juice drips through. Add more apple to jelly bag as space permits. Continue until you have collected 2 cups of strained juice.
9. Heat juice in a heavy enameled or stainless-steel pot. Stir in sugar gradually until dissolved.
9. Simmer syrup until it falls in 2 heavy drops from the side of a spoon (about 205°F on a candy thermometer).
10. Add oranges and lemon juice. Simmer for 30 minutes, or until orange peel tastes sweet. (Remember, there will always be a delicate edge of bitterness in homemade marmalade.)
11. Turn up heat and boil rapidly for 1–2 minutes, removing white foam that forms on surface.
12. Continue to boil until marmalade is thick and falls from the side of a spoon in a single drop (220–222°F). Remove from heat. Stir in rose water.
13. Pour into sterilized jelly glasses. If you intend to store marmalade unrefrigerated, cool and cover with a layer of paraffin.

YIELD: 3 cups

*Names of suppliers of jelly bags and frames may be obtained from Leisure Technology, 1615 West River Road, North Minneapolis, Minnesota 55411. In New York City, jelly bags may be purchased at the Bridge Company, 212 East 52nd Street.

Paste of Apples and Pears

First having scalded your Fruit in Water, 'till they become soft, then let them be drained, passed thro' a Sieve, and dried over the Fire, but Care must be taken to stir them with a Spatula from time to time, both on the Bottom and round about to prevent their burning. When the Paste slips off from the Bottom and Sides of the Pan, remove it from the Fire, and cause some Sugar to be greatly feather'd or crack'd, which must be well incorporated with it, allowing a Pound of Fruit for the like Quantity of Sugar. Afterwards, set your Paste again over the Fire, to simmer, and dress it as the others in Moulds, or upon Slates setting all at the same time into the Stove to be dried.

The Whole Duty of a Woman

Apple-Pear Candies. These little fruit candies are very festive and go nicely with most any eighteenth-century "desart."

2 large cooking apples, cored and quartered
2 large cooking pears, cored and quartered
3 cups sugar

1. Boil apples and pears in water to cover until they are very soft. Drain.
2. Pass fruit through a strainer or the fine blade of a food mill.
3. In a heavy saucepan, cook fruit purée over moderate heat, stirring frequently, until mixture is very dry and a spoon drawn across it will make a path at the bottom of the pan.
4. Meanwhile, in a heavy pot, dissolve sugar in $\frac{1}{2}$ cup water. Boil until syrup reaches the soft-crack stage (290°F on a candy thermometer). You may test doneness by dropping a small quantity of syrup into ice water; it will separate into threads which when removed from the water will bend (not break).
5. Pour syrup into fruit purée, stirring vigorously.
6. Simmer, stirring frequently, until mixture is very thick (about 1 hour). Be careful not to scorch the bottom, but if you do, quickly scrape off the burnt section. A flame tamer placed under the pot helps considerably.
7. Drop fruit paste in small spoonfuls on waxed paper. Dry for 3–4 days at room temperature, or until candies are no longer sticky to the touch. Flip candies over every 12 hours.
8. Store in an airtight container.

NOTE: You may, as the original recipe suggests, dry the candies in a very slow oven (150°F). Place 1 inch apart on a baking sheet covered with baking parchment and bake about 12 hours, or until candies are no longer sticky to the touch. However, if your oven is unpredictable and has bursts of energy, you run the risk of caramelizing the sugar.

YIELD: about 3 dozen candies

A Very Good Whipp'd Syllabub

Take a Pint of Cream, a Glass of Sack, the Whites of two Eggs, a Quarter of Pound of fine Sugar, and with a whisk whip and beat it to a Froth very well, scum it and put it in your Glasses for that Purpose.

John Middleton, *Five Hundred New Receipts*

Whipped Syllabub. The earliest syllabubs were made by milking a cow directly into a basin of cider or ale and leaving the mixture to sit until a soft curd formed on top. Special syllabub pots with spouts were made for serving this semi-liquid dessert.

By the late seventeenth century, syllabub was often made of cream beaten to a froth and set atop a small glass of wine. In later years it became more common to whip all of the ingredients together, as in the recipe below.

This dessert is especially appropriate for those people who eat cake as an excuse to have some whipped cream.

1 cup heavy cream, chilled
2 tablespoons sugar
$\frac{1}{4}$ cup plus 2 tablespoons dry sherry
white of 1 large egg

1. In a bowl, whip cream and sugar.
2. Stir sherry into whipped cream.
3. In a small bowl, whip egg white until it forms stiff peaks.
4. Gently fold egg white into whipped cream.
5. Spoon small amounts of syllabub into cordial or sherry glasses.
6. Chill at least 2 hours before serving.

SERVES 4–6

To Make Cream Cheese with Old Cheshire

Take a pound and a half of old cheshire-cheese, shave it all very thin, then put it in a mortar and add to it a quarter of an ounce of mace beaten fine and sifted, half a pound of fresh butter, and a glass of sack; mix and beat all these together till they are perfectly incorporated; then put it in a pot what thickness you please, and cut it out in slices for cream cheese, and serve it with the desert.

Eliza Smith, *The Compleat Housewife*

Potted Cheese. Cheshire is one of the oldest English cheeses; in fact, it is said that the Romans built the city of Chester so they could control the district where this cheese was made.

Surplus and aging cheeses were often potted so that their moisture and freshness could be preserved. This potted cheese is delicately spiced and makes a very pleasant finale to an eighteenth-century meal.

180

1½ pounds Cheshire cheese, finely grated
½ pound butter at room temperature
½ cup plus 2 tablespoons dry sherry
scant ¼ teaspoon mace

1. In a bowl, combine ingredients. Work them together with the back of a spoon.
2. Place mixture in an earthenware dish with a tight-fitting lid. (Alternatively, you may wish to fold waxed paper around mixture and press into the form of a loaf.)
3. Chill thoroughly.
4. Serve in slices on individual dessert plates.

NOTE: It is particularly nice to serve this cheese with apples or pears.

SERVES 6–8

OF BRANDY, PUNCH, SACK POSSITT AND A CURE FOR THE BITE OF A MAD DOG

To Make Lemmon Brandy

Take the thin upper rinds of two Lemmons sufused in three pints of brandy twenty-four hours then boyle a pinte of water with near half a pound of sugar & put it hot to your brandy & Lemmons: then stop it close & let it stand three or four hours then filtre it through a brown paper.

Elizabeth Wainwright, *The Receipt Book of a Lady of the Reign of Queen Anne*

OF ALL THE SPIRITS imported into England during the eighteenth century, brandy was the most expensive and most esteemed. In *A Friendly Admonition to the Drinkers of Brandy* (1733), physicians warned that "these distilled spiritous liquors, which are inflamed by repeated distillation are, in a manner, direct poison to human bodies," but it was to no avail.

Home-distilled brandies and those of inferior quality were often steeped with fruits or citrus peel. Here is an easy recipe which you might like to try, but do not hesitate to serve any type of store-bought brandy at the end of your eighteenth-century dinner.

2 large lemons
2 quarts brandy
2 cups water
½ cup sugar

1. Remove peel from lemons (see directions, p. 54).
2. In a large decanter or suitable container, store brandy and lemon peel for 24 hours.
3. In a saucepan, boil water and sugar. When syrup has cooled slightly, pour it into the brandy. (Make certain it is not so hot that it will break the decanter.)
4. Cover or cork the decanter. Set aside for an additional 4-5 hours.
5. Pour through a strainer. Store for use.

YIELD: 2½ quarts

185

To Make a Good Punch

In order to make a good punch you must take the juice of four lemons, or two bitter oranges for a bowl containing three pots, this drink being always made in a big china bowl. You must have a lump of sugar the size of your fist, according to taste and whether you like it sweet or not. Next add old brandy from Nantes, in France, which must be mellow; this again to suit your taste. The best punch is made from two liquors that are brought from the Indies—one of them is rum, the other arak. Rum is a sort of Brandy made in the West Indies with the dregs or refuse of the sugar cane. It is stronger than brandy, so you must add less of it to the punch. Arak comes from the East Indies, and it is extracted from rice. This is a sweet liquor, and you must add almost as much of it to the punch as you would of spring water.

César de Saussure, *A Foreign View of England*

TRAVELERS were fascinated by English punch, and Saussure even goes so far as to give a recipe for its preparation. Here is a simple punch adapted from his instructions. The following ingredients will serve six, but you may double or triple the amounts if you plan to serve a large quantity in a punchbowl.

6 jiggers (scant $\frac{1}{2}$ cup) rum
3 jiggers (scant $\frac{1}{4}$ cup) brandy
1 tablespoon (or more) sugar
juice of 3 small lemons (about $\frac{1}{2}$ cup)
ice
cold water or soda water

1. Combine all ingredients except water. Shake well with ice.
2. Strain into 6 seven-ounce glasses.
3. Fill each glass to the top with water.

SERVES 6

To Make a Sack Possitt

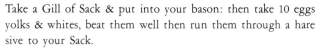

Take a Gill of Sack & put into your bason: then take 10 eggs yolks & whites, beat them well then run them through a hare sive to your Sack.

Sweeten your eggs & sack then set it on the fire to thicken stiring it till you think it be thick enough; then boyle a quart of good cream & power it as high as you can to your sack & eggs & stir it easily together. So let it stand a while & send it up. Looke it do not Curdel.

Elizabeth Wainwright, *The Receipt Book of a Lady of the Reign of Queen Anne*

Sack Posset. This soothing drink was usually served in a small, two-handled, silver posset cup. These cups often came with covers, for the sack and warmed cream had to be set aside until a soft curd formed. When Sophia arrives at Upton Inn and discovers that Tom has been and gone, she requests sack posset "made very small and thin" to soothe her shattered nerves. Sack posset makes a fine nightcap.

2 large eggs, well beaten
$\frac{1}{4}$ cup dry sherry
1–2 tablespoons sugar
1 cup heavy cream

1. Combine eggs, sherry, and sugar in the top of a double boiler.
2. Set over a pot of hot but not boiling water and cook, stirring frequently, until mixture thickens. Do not let mixture boil or it will curdle.
3. In a saucepan, bring cream to a boil.
4. Let cream cool slightly, then whisk into sherry mixture.
5. Pour into small mugs or soup bowls and serve.

SERVES 4

189

A Certain Cure for the Bite of a Mad Dog. By Dr. Mead

THE PHENOMENAL success of Mrs. Glasse's *The Art of Cookery* has never been satisfactorily explained, but some critics believe it was due to her timely inclusion of "A Certain Cure for the Bite of a Mad Dog. By Dr. Mead" as the final chapter of her book.

A widespread paranoia among the English during the eighteenth century is described by Oliver Goldsmith in *Citizen of the World* (1760–1762):

> A dread of mad dogs is the epidemic terror which now prevails; and the whole nation is at present actually groaning under the malignity of its influence. The people sally from their houses with that circumspection which is prudent in such as expect a mad dog at every turning. The physician publishes his prescription, the beadle prepares his halter, and a few of unusual bravery arm themselves with boots and buff gloves, in order to face the enemy if he should offer to attack them.

The account of the fate of one victim bitten by a mad dog is so embellished, according to Goldsmith,

> that by the time it has arrived in town the lady is described, with wide eyes, foaming mouth, running mad upon all-fours, barking like a dog, biting her servants, and at last smothered between two beds by the advice of her doctors; while the mad mastiff is in the mean time ranging the whole country over, slavering at the mouth, and seeking whom he may devour.*

Dr. Mead was the author of many medical treatises. Although somewhat notorious for fighting a duel with a man who publicly disagreed with his theories, Mead was sufficiently respected to be called in for consultation at Queen Anne's deathbed.

Mead's prescription, as quoted by Mrs. Glasse in 1747, follows:

*Oliver Goldsmith, *Miscellaneous Works,* edited by James Prior, vol. 2 (New York, 1857), pp. 288–91.

A Certain Cure for the Bite of a Mad Dog

Let the patient be blooded at the arm nine or ten ounces. Take of the herb called in Latin *lichen cinereus terrestris,* in English, ash-coloured, ground liverwort, cleaned, dried, and powdered, half an ounce. Of black pepper, powdered, two drachms. Mix these well together, and divide the powder into four doses, one of which must be taken every morning fasting, for four mornings successively, in half a pint of cow's milk warm. After these four doses are taken, the patient must go into the cold bath, or a cold spring or river every morning fasting for a month. He must be dipped all over, but not to stay in (with his head above water) longer than half a minute, if the water be very cold. After this he must go in three times a week for a fortnight longer.

One can't help but wonder which would prove more harmful, the bite or the cure. . . .

The same Animal which hath the Honour to have some Part of his Flesh eaten at the Table of a Duke, may perhaps be degraded in another Part, and some of his Limbs gibbeted, as it were, in the vilest Stall in Town. Where then lies the Difference between the Food of the Nobleman and the Porter, if both are at dinner on the same Ox or Calf, but in the seasoning, the dressing, the garnishing, and the setting forth?

Henry Fielding, *Tom Jones*

BILLS OF FARE: *Then*

THE FOLLOWING SUMMER menu suggested by Eliza Smith in *The Compleat Housewife* is addressed to housewives of modest means. Mrs. Smith almost exclusively recommends those foods which foreign travelers regard as typical for gentlemen as well as the "middling sort," with the notable exception of a *white fricacy.* Asterisks indicate recipes which may be found in *Dinner with Tom Jones.*

FIRST COURSE:
A Soop remove Dish of Fish*
Orange Pudding
White Fricacy*
A Venison Pasty
Tongue & Colliflower
Bacon and Bean
A Chine of Mutton

SECOND COURSE:
Chickens* or Partridge
Veal Sweet Breads
Marrow Pasties
Young Peas
Roasted Pigeons
Young Rabbits

DESSERT: Sweet Meat Tarts of all sorts*

LADY GRISELL-BAILLIE, a well-educated aristocrat, recorded one hundred and seventy "Bills of Fair" in a notebook of that title. She and those of her social circle generally maintained a minimum of eight cooks to prepare food for their large households. Here is the menu for one of the meals that Lady Baillie enjoyed.

Sunday, Christenmas 1715, w^t 9 of our frinds 14 at table in all

Plumb patage with sagoe and a few frute*

relief minsht pys*

fricascy chickens*   Bra[w]n   plumb puden*

rost bief

2

a rost goos

col[d] toung   Bra[w]n   oyster loves

Desert

Ratafia cream

butter and chease*   sillibubs*   Jacolet walnuts and almonds

aples   stewd pears

chestons   Jellys   butter and chease

BILLS OF FARE: *Now*

IN PLANNING menus for eighteenth-century meals, avoid serving more than two dishes that are sweet or rich and creamy. For example, if you plan to make plum pottage and potato pudding, have a fairly simple entrée and dessert. You may appropriately substitute roasted or boiled meat accompanied with a sauce, *cullis,* or *ragoo* for any of the entrées below. All of the puddings may successfully be served as an accompaniment to fish or meat, but plum, apple, and fruit puddings would also make fine desserts.

LUNCHEON FOR FOUR

Carrot Soup
Mushroom Tart
Salmogundy
Strawberry Fool
Tea

DINNER FOR SIX

Georgian Salad
Onion Soup
Mushroom Tart
Stuffed Veal or Lamb Roast
Potato Pudding
Pineapple Tart
Potted Cheese
Wine, Brandy, or Punch

DINNER FOR EIGHT

Plum Pottage
Fried Eel
Cheshire Pork Pie   Mutton Stew
Artichoke Pudding   Pickled Red Cabbage
Westminster Fool   Apple-Pear Candies
Potted Cheese
Wine, Brandy, or Punch

DINNER FOR TEN

Georgian Salad
Almond Soup
Savory Toasts   Stuffed Mushrooms
Chicken Fricassee   Mincemeat Pie
Cauliflower Pudding   Fried Celery
Chocolate Tart   Ratafia Puffs
Potted Cheese
Wine, Brandy, or Punch

Glossary

alegar — sour ale; vinegar formed by the fermentation of ale

arak — arrack; an alcoholic beverage resembling rum in taste and distilled from the fermented juice of the coconut palm or from a fermented mash of rice and molasses

bloomage — blooms; blossoms

bohea — the finest Chinese black tea

brawn — the flesh of a boar collared and boiled, then pickled or potted

broum buds — broom buds; flower buds which were pickled and used, like capers, for flavoring

calipash — that part of the turtle next to the upper shell containing a green gelatinous substance

calipee — that part of the turtle next to the lower shell containing a yellow gelatinous substance

capers — the pickled flower buds of a shrub; used for flavoring

carmine — a red or crimson pigment obtained from the red dyestuff cochineal

cheafing dish — chafing dish; a vessel intended to hold food being warmed, or the fuel it was warmed by

cheston — a species of plum so named for its resemblance to chestnuts

chine of mutton — saddle of mutton

citron — a fruit with a very thick white inner skin enclosing a small amount of sour pulp. The peel is candied by soaking in brine and then preserving in sugar.

clarified butter — butter which has been melted over low heat and left to stand so that the milk solids settle to the bottom. The clarified butter may then be poured off the top.

codling — a young or small cod

coffin — pie pastry shell; usually large and freestanding

colap — collop; a small piece or slice of meat

collaring — rolling up a piece of meat or fish often around a stuffing and then binding it tightly with cloth or string

cowcumber — cucumber

cowslip pudding — a custard-like pudding flavored with the wild cowslip flower

cullis — a strong broth usually made from meat or fowl; used as a base for sauces and as a nourishing food for invalids (Beef tea is a well-known example of the latter.)

currey the Indian way — In Mrs. Glasse's recipe, chicken is stewed with onions, turmeric, ginger, pepper, cream, and lemon juice.

delf — delftware; glazed pottery which originated in Delft, Holland

dish of tea — tea with milk and sugar drunk from a small porcelain bowl (like the teacups used in Chinese restaurants today)

dram — a small draught of cordial; approximately one eighth of a fluid ounce

draw — to extract blood and organs from the cavity of a fish or animal

faggot of herbs — *bouquet garni;* a bouquet of fresh herbs such as thyme, rosemary, savory, or parsley, tied together and cooked in soups and stews to impart flavor

farce, fierce, force — to stuff

farce, forcing — stuffing

flackes — flakes

forc'd meat — forcemeat; finely ground meat used for stuffings and sausages, and sometimes for meatballs

French roll — a small round of bread whose dough has been enriched with butter and eggs

friggassee — stew

gally-pot — gallipot; a glazed earthenware pot, often tall and narrow; used for molding jellies and for storing gravies and pickles

gill — a liquid measure; one half of a standard pint during most of the eighteenth century

grass — asparagus

gross — coarse

gumboodge — gamboge; a gum resin with a bright yellow color

harrico — stew

hoop — a round cake pan

household bread — bread of mixed grain; generally eaten by peasants

hyson — the finest Chinese green tea

jacolet walnuts and almonds — chocolate-coated nuts

Jamaica pepper, Jamaka pepper — allspice

jigger — a liquid measure; one and a half fluid ounces

jill — gill; one half of a standard pint

jugging — tightly packing food into an earthenware jug and then cooking it by immersing the jug in boiling water

julep — a liquid sweetened with syrup or sugar

kernel — the inner, soft part of a fruit pit, usually apricot

kibbob of lamb — skewered, roasted lamb

liquor — liquid

leer — lear; a thick sauce

manchett — fine-quality white bread

megrim — migraine headache

mould — knead into firm dough

muske — a substance derived from a small sac under the skin of the abdomen in the male musk deer; used to perfume foods. The musk seed, which has a similar odor, is nowadays used instead.

nonpareils — sugar-coated candies which "have no equal" (from the French *non pareil,* without equal)

nostrum — recipe; used pejoratively to refer to quack medicines

olio — a highly spiced stew of meat and vegetables

outlandish — from another land; foreign

oyster loves — French rolls or loaves of bread stuffed with stewed oysters

paste — pie pastry

patty — a little pie or pasty

patty-pans — small tin pans in which pies or pasties were baked

peck — a unit of dry measure equal to one fourth of a bushel, or eight quarts

penny-loaf — a small loaf of bread which was sold for a penny. The weight of the loaf varied according to the price and quality of wheat used for the dough.

pill — peel

pipin, pippin — a variety of dessert apple with a yellow or greenish-yellow skin

pipkin — a small pot, usually glazed earthenware or stoneware

postalia nuts — pistachio nuts

pottage — a thick soup which often contained pieces of meat and vegetable

prunella salt — sal prunella, a preparation of saltpeter

quarter — eight bushels or twenty-eight pounds

race — root; generally used in reference to ginger

ragoo — ragout; a stew

ramkin — toasted bread covered with a meat-and-cheese paste

rasp — grate

ratafea, ratafee, ratifee — ratafia; apricot kernels or bitter almonds, or their flavor

red sage — a variety of common garden sage

remove — the act of taking away a dish or dishes at a meal in order to put others in their place; a dish thus removed

Rhenish wine — Rhine wine

sack — sherry

sack possitt — sack posset; a thick, soothing drink of sherry, eggs, and warmed cream

sago — a farinaceous substance prepared from the pith of the palm tree and resembling tapioca; imported from the West Indies

salamander — a circular iron plate, heated and then held over cooked food to brown the top

salmogundy — salmagundy; a salad plate consisting of chopped or sliced meats, anchovies, hard-boiled eggs, greens, etc., that are arranged in layers for flavor and color contrast

salsify — "oyster plant"; an edible white root likened to the oyster in taste; eaten as a vegetable

sapor — taste; flavor

scorzonera — a fleshy black-skinned root with white flesh; eaten as a vegetable

sippets — sops; pieces of fried or toasted bread

skirret — a species of water parsnip no longer cultivated on a large scale

slates — thin flat slabs of rock used as baking sheets

smalt — deep blue glass used as a pigment for coloring when finely pulverized

sops — pieces of fried or toasted bread

soup meagre — literally, soup without flesh (meat); a rich vegetable soup

suet — the crumbly fat deposited around the kidneys and loins of cattle and sheep

sugar nipper — a scissor-like implement used to slice pieces of sugar from the loaf

sweet breads — the pancreas or thymus of an animal; the latter is preferred

sweet-meats — fruit or peel preserved by candying

syllabub — a combination of sweetened wine and cream served as a drink or dessert

tansey — an egg-based dish, fried or baked; originally colored green and flavored with the herb tansy

verijuice — verjuice; the juice of unripened grapes or crab apples

wafering iron — a wrought-iron implement fashioned like blacksmiths' tongs, but with the jaws made of two flat discs four to five inches in diameter, the inner surface being covered with incised designs; used for making wafers

Bibliography of Primary Sources

Code: AC = Author's collection; BL = British Library; CU = Columbia University; NYPL = New York Public Library; SA = Szathmary Archives

Unless otherwise noted, references are to first editions printed in London. Those books whose locations are not given in parentheses may be found in the New York Public Library.

I. **Printed cookbooks and volumes containing a substantial selection of recipes:**

Adam's Luxury, and Eve's Cookery: or, The Kitchen-Garden Display'd, 1744.

Atkyns, Arabella (pseud.), *The Family Magazine*, 1741.

Bailey, N. (attrib.), *Dictionarium Rusticum & Urbanicum: or, A Dictionary of All Sorts of Country Affairs*, 1704.
_____, *Dictionarium Domesticum*, 1736. (BL)

Battam, A., *A Collection of Scarce and Valuable Receipts*, 1750. (BL)

Bradley, R., *The Country Housewife and Lady's Director*, 1727. (BL)

Bradshaw, Penelope, *Bradshaw's Valuable Family Jewel*, 10th ed., 1748. (BL)

Carter, Charles, *The Complete Practical Cook*, 1730.

———, *The Compleat City and Country Cook: or, Accomplish'd Housewife*, 3rd ed., 1732.

———, *The London and Country Cook: or, Accomplished Housewife*, 3rd ed., 1749.

Cleland, Elizabeth, *A New and Easy Method of Cookery*, Edinburgh, 1755.

The Complete Family Piece: and, Country Gentleman, and Farmer's Best Guide, 1737. (*SA*)

The Country Magazine, June 1736– February 1737.

Eales, Mary, *Mrs. Mary Eales's Receipts*, 1718.

———, *The Compleat Confectioner: or, The Art of Candying and Preserving in its Utmost Perfection*, 3rd ed., 1742.

Ellis, William, *The Country Housewife's Family Companion*, 1750.

Evelyn, John, *Acetaria: A Discourse of Sallets*, 1699. (BL)

Fairfax, Arabella, *The Family's Best Friend: or, The Whole Art of Cookery made Plain and Easy*, 5th ed., 1753.

[Glasse, Hannah], *The Art of Cookery, made Plain and Easy. By a Lady*, 1747.

———, *The Compleat Confectioner*, Dublin, 1762.

The Good Housewife: or, Cookery Reformed, 2nd ed., 1756.

Hall, T., *The Queen's Royal Cookery*, 1709.

Harrison, Sarah, *The House-keeper's Pocket-Book; and Compleat Family Cook*, 3rd ed., Dublin, 1738.

Howard, Henry, *England's Newest Way in All Sorts of Cookery, Pastry and Pickles*, 3rd ed., 1710. (BL)

J. (W.), *The True Gentlewoman's Delight*, 1707. (BL)

Jackson, Sarah, *The Director: or, Young Woman's Best Companion*, 1755.

Johnson, Mary, *Madam Johnson's Present: or, The Best Instructions for Young Women*, 1754.

Kettilby, Mary, *A Collection of Above Three Hundred Receipts in Cookery, Physick and Surgery*, 2nd ed., 1719.

Kidder, Edward, *E. Kidder's Receipts of Pastry and Cookery*, c. 1740.

La Chapelle, Vincent, *The Modern Cook*, 3rd ed., 1744.

Lamb, Patrick, *Royal Cookery: or, The Complete Court-Cook*, 1710.

Massiolot, François, *The Court and Country Cook*, translated from the French, 1702.

Middleton, John, *Five Hundred New Receipts*, revised by Henry Howard, 1734.

Moxon, Elizabeth, *English Housewifery*, 5th ed., Leeds, c. 1750.

Nott, John, *The Cook's and Confectioner's Dictionary: or, The Accomplish'd Housewife's Companion*, 1723.

The Pastry-Cook's Vade-Mecum, 1705. (BL)

A Present for a Servant-Maid, 1743. (BL)

Salmon, William, *The Family-Dictionary*, 1705.

S[mith], E[liza], *The Compleat Housewife: or, Accomplished Gentlewoman's Companion*, 2nd ed., 1728. (BL); 15th ed., 1753. (AC)

Smith, Robert, *Court Cookery: or, The Compleat English Cook*, 1723.

The Summer's Amusement: or, The Young Ladies Companion, 1746.

The Whole Duty of a Woman, 1737.

II. Manuscript cookery books:

Fleming, Alice, 1702. (AC)
Moult, Daniel, c. 1700. (BL Sloane 3817)
Nicholson, Anne, 1707. (BL Additional 30, 244)
Pemberton, Penelope, 1716. (SA)
Sloane, Elizabeth, 1711. (BL Additional 29, 739)

III. Modern editions of eighteenth-century manuscript cookery books:

Astry, Diana, *Diana Astry's Recipe Book,* c. 1700, edited by Bette Stitt, The Publications of the Bedfordshire Historical Records Society, vol. 37, 1956.

A Book of Simples, edited by H. W. Lewer, 1908.

Cook, Ann, *Ann Cook and Friend,* edited by Regula Burnet, 1936.

In an Eighteenth Century Kitchen, edited by Dennis Rhodes, 1968.

Newington, Thomas, *A Butler's Recipe Book,* edited by Philip James, Cambridge, 1935.

Recipes from a Ladies Diary, 1718, Department of Printing, Exeter College, 1976.

Wainwright, Elizabeth, *The Receipt Book of a Lady of the*

Reign of Queen Anne, Hampshire, 1931.

IV. Related works printed in the eighteenth century:

Cheyne, George, *An Essay of Health and Long Life,* 5th ed., 1734. (SA)

Duncan, Daniel, *Wholesome Advise Against the Abuse of Hot Liquors, particularly of Coffee, Chocolate, Tea, Brandy, and Strong-Waters,* 1706.

Dodd, J. S., *An Essay towards the Natural History of the Herring,* 1752.

The Female Spectator, vol. 6, 1745.

King, William, *The Art of Cookery in Imitation of Horace's Art of Poetry,* 1730. (SA)

Langley, Batty, *New Principles of Gardening,* 1728. (BL)
————, *Pomona: or, the Fruit Garden Illustrated,* 1729. (BL)

[Laroon, Marcellus], *The Cryes of the City of London,* 1692. (BL)

Lemery, Louis, *A Treatise of all Sorts of Foods,* translated by D. Hay, 1745.

Switzer, Stephen, *Iconographia Rustica,* 1718. (CU)
————, *The Practical Kitchen Gardner,* 1727. (BL)

Waldron, John, *A Satyr against Tea: or, Ovington's Essay upon the Nature and Qualities of Tea Dissected, and Burlesq'd,* Dublin, 1733. (BL)

Suggestions for Further Reading

Additional texts of interest may be found in the notes to the introduction.

Botsford, Jay Barrett, *English Society in the Eighteenth Century,* New York, 1965. A sophisticated, very well documented study of the effects of overseas trade and exploration on English society. Of special interest are the sections "The National Diet," "Rise of the Middle Class and Levelling of Social Distinctions," and "The Refinement of Taste and Manners."

Fussell, G. E. and K. R., *The English Countrywoman: A Farmhouse Social History A.D. 1500–1900,* London, 1953. Because it focuses on the woman's duties, this thoroughly researched study furnishes much interesting information on food and drink. All of the Fussells' many books on or related to agricultural history are recommended; they generally have extensive bibliographies.

Grisell-Baillie, Lady, *The Household Book of Lady Grisell-Baillie: 1692–1733,* edited by Robert Scott-Moncrieff, Scottish History Society, Edinburgh, 1911. Household books provide valuable insights into the workings of daily life, and this one is no exception. The family lives in Edinburgh, London, Bath, and on the Continent, and the records show the range of food prices and wages in these different locations over a forty-year period. There are valuable sections on "Bills of Fare" and "Directions to Servants."

Honey, W. B., *English Pottery and Porcelain,* London, 1933. This concise history of English ceramic art provides a good introduction to the development of traditional earthenware, stoneware, and porcelain from the Middle Ages through the nineteenth century. There are good illustrations of eighteenth century tableware, and the volume contains a useful bibliography.

McKearin, Helen, "Sweetmeats in Splendor: eighteenth-century desserts and their dressing out," *Antiques* 67 (March 1955), 216–25. A most valuable article documenting the century's interest in elaborate desserts. The article includes many plates from period cookbooks which demonstrate how desserts were supposed to be set out.

Oman, Charles, *English Domestic Silver,* London, 1968. A former curator of the Victoria and Albert Museum, Oman has gathered examples of silver cups, bowls, chocolate pots, tea caddies, etc., from their earliest production through the eighteenth century.

Oxford, A. W., *English Cookery Books to 1850,* London, 1913. Although incomplete, Oxford's is the best bibliography for the study of historical English cookery. A reprint of this edition has just been published.

The Oxford Book of Food Plants, illustrated by B. E. Nicholson, Oxford, 1975. This exquisitely illustrated volume will show you what some of the strange fruits and vegetables you've been hearing about look like.

Trevelyan, G. M., *Illustrated English Social History:* vol. 3,

Middlesex, 1960. Trevelyan provides a general backdrop of social history during the eighteenth century. His flowing text is so heavily illustrated with contemporary art that you feel as if you're reading a picture book.

Wroth, Warwick, *The London Pleasure Gardens of the Eighteenth Century,* London, 1896. This thorough and well-documented study is the *magnum opus* on the subject. Period illustrations of the gardens are breathtaking, and the author relates many amusing anecdotes which bring the gaiety of the gardens into the reader's living room.

Notes on the Illustrations

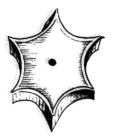

The lively imbibers on the cover and the sketches of country life which appear throughout the text are by Thomas Rowlandson (1756-1827) from *Outlines of Figures, Landscapes, and Cattle,* London, 1790-1792 (The Elisha Whittelsey Collection, The Elisha Whittelsey Fund, 1953. 53.638.27,59.533.1017). The drawing of "The Squire's Kitchen" on page 37 is also by Rowlandson (Harris Brisbane Dick Fund, 1941. 41.77.2). "A Bird's Eye View of Convent Garden" on the front endpapers and "A Bird's Eye View of Smithfield Market" on the back endpapers were drawn by Rowlandson and A. C. Pugin, aquatinted by Black, London, 1811 (The Elisha Whittelsey Collection, The Elisha Whittelsey Fund, 1959. 59.533.1082,1145).

The portrait of Henry Fielding on page 12 is an etching by William Hogarth (1697-1764) made in 1792 (Harris Brisbane Dick Fund, 1917. 17.3.756-1674).

The illustrations on pages 21, 94, and 160 are from a cookbook, *The Lady's Companion,* volume 1, 5th edition, London, 1751 (The Elisha Whittelsey Collection, The Elisha Whittelsey Fund, 1960. 60.511.5).

Index to the Recipes

206

LORNA J. SASS is a native New Yorker whose interest in historical cookery was sparked by the serendipitous discovery of medieval manuscript recipes in Columbia University's Butler Library. Having survived an initial series of disastrous culinary experiments, she found herself hooked to the taste of cubebs, galingale, and grains of paradise, and after a few years wrote her first book, *To the King's Taste,* based on a cookery manuscript from the household of Richard II, dated c. 1390. Through this work she became fascinated with the study of food as an aspect of social history and went on to investigate a slightly later period, producing *To the Queen's Taste,* a companion cookbook on the Elizabethan Age.

Lorna Sass has been a member of the Queens College English Department, and currently teaches writing at Columbia University, where she is completing a doctorate in medieval literature. She gives evening courses on the history of gastronomy and runs workshops in historical cookery on college campuses and at her Manhattan cooking school, Feasts Unlimited.